NO PEACEFUL WAY:

Chile's Struggle For Dignity

Gary MacEoin

NO PEACEFUL WAY:

Chile's Struggle For Dignity

SHEED AND WARD, INC.
Subsidiary of United Press Syndicate

IBSN-8362-0569-3

Library of Congress Card No. 74-1531

A particular debt is gratefully acknowledged to Reverend William Wipfler, head of the Latin American Working Group of the National Council of Churches of Christ in the United States, for his encouragement of the project, and for his generous sharing of vast knowledge and sympathetic understanding of the subject. Both he and his associate, Alison Raphael, also enabled me to consult vast resources of published and unpublished materials otherwise not easily accessible.

Others who read major portions of the text and enriched it with corrections, evaluations and suggestions include Thomas Bamat, John Pollock and Dale Johnson of the department of sociology, Livingston College, Rutgers University, and David Barkin of New York University.

Christopher Roper, coeditor of *Latin America Review of Books*, and Richard Gott, general editor of the Latin American Library of Penguin Books and Latin American editor of *The Guardian*, both of London, helped substantially with the Bibliography.

iv

GLOSSARY

AIFLD: American Institute for Free Labor Development.

Callampa: slum

Campamento: improved slum, workingclass community

CODELCO: Corporación del Cobre (Chilean Copper Corporation)

Comandos Comunales: neighborhood commands or committees

Consejo Comunal: neighborhood board

Cordones Industriales: industrial belts

CORFO: Corporación de Fomento (State Development Corporation)

CUPROCH: Confederación Unica de Profesionales (Central Confederation of Professional Workers)

CUT: Confederación Unica de Trabajadores (Central Labor Confederation)

DC: Democracia Cristiana (Christian Democracy)

FDU: Federación Democrática Unida (United Democratic Federation), a combination of DC and PN in opposition to UP coalition

FIN: Fuente de Información Norteamericana (Source of North American Information) a research and publishing group of North Americans in Santiago.

Gremio: any kind of association, including labor unions and employer protection groups.

MIR: Movimiento Izquierdista Revolucionario (Movement of Revolutionary Left).

MAPU: Movimiento de Acción Popular Unido (United Movement of Popular Action)

MIC: Movimiento Izquierdista Cristiano (Movement of Christian Left)

Operación Djakarta: Operation Jakarta, codename of plot to overthrow UP coalition

Patria y Libertad: Fatherland and Freedom, rightwing vigilante organization

v

PC: Partido Comunista (Communist Party)
PDS: Partido Democrático Social (Social Democratic Party)
PN: Partido Nacional (National Party), extreme rightwing
Población: same as campamento
Poblador: resident of a población
PR: Partido Radical (Radical Party)
Protección Comunal (Neighborhood protection), a rightwing vigilante group
PS: Partido Socialista (Socialist Party)
Soberanía, Orden y Libertad: Sovereignty, Order and Freedom, a rightwing vigilante group
SNA: Sociedad Nacional de Agricultores (National Society of Landowners)
SOFOFA: Sociedad de Fomento Fabril (National Manufacturers' Association)
UP: Unidad Popular (Popular Unity)

CONTENTS

INTRODUCTION

Chile in 1970 embarked on a new experiment in man's long search for a better society, when Salvador Allende, a 62-year-old medical doctor, took office as president with a mandate to lead his country to socialism by constitutional methods. The world was shocked and disheartened three years later when Chile's armed forces, reputedly nonpolitical and committed to constitutionality, repudiated the constitution and broke a long tradition by resorting to violence in which President Allende and thousands died.

The challenge to the conscience of mankind grew in subsequent weeks, as the victorious military behaved like "occupation forces in a foreign country," to use the description of a Chilean who had been an outspoken critic of Allende and had welcomed the army's intervention to oust him.[1] They suspended indefinitely the civil rights of all citizens and residents, engaged in mass executions, abolished Congress, outlawed many political parties and put all the others on inactive status, indulged in an orgy of book burning, named generals to run government departments and the universities, and set out to remake society in the molds of a fascist dictatorship.

1

These events are of most immediate significance to
Chileans, especially to the two-thirds of the country's ten
million citizens who are being thrust back—at least temporarily—to their traditional have-not condition after a brief
but real participation in the decision-making processes of
their society, a sense of dignity as men and women, and
reasonable access to the food and other basic commodities
produced in Chile by the common efforts of all. But this
Chilean experience has a much wider meaning for mankind. Its attempt to find a new road to economic and
social well-being aroused the hopes and anticipations of
vast numbers of people in all parts of the world who know
that man has recently achieved such control of his environment that he can here and now provide decent living levels
to the two-thirds of mankind who lack them. The brutal
closing of that road must force all these expectant millions
to re-evaluate their assumptions, will undoubtedly drive
many of them to more extreme and violence-prone stands.

For Latin America the experience of Chile is particularly important, because Chile is in many respects a micro-
cosm of the hemisphere. Here one can see, in a form more
evolved than in most other countries, the combined impact
of the earlier history of colonialism and the subsequent
history of neocolonialism under nominally independent
political regimes. Colonialism created the basic pattern of a
small group monopolizing power and using it to extract
from the oppressed majority more than a reasonable share
of the wealth created by their common efforts. A century
of dependence on mining as the basis of international trade
and major source of foreign exchange had fully integrated
the dominant minority into the international structures of
domination and dependence. In the same way as the oligarchy within Chile through its monopoly of domestic power
secured for itself an inequitable share of the nation's
production, so the powerful nations which monopolize
world power secured for themselves an inequitable share of

2

the benefits extracted from the soil of Chile to satisfy the industrial needs of those rich nations. At this level, however, there was a significant difference. While Chile was being despoiled, the oligarchs did not suffer, because their monopoly of domestic power—supported to the extent needed by the massive power of the external associates— enabled them to pass the entire burden to the oppressed majority of Chileans. These are institutionalized relationships. No foreign or domestic power-holder orders that people should go hungry. It is the formulation and manipulation of public policy that determines that some luxuriate in abundance while others starve. The difference results from decisions on wages and prices, on the availability to some on credit denied to others, of the direction and level of investment, on the privileges granted outside capital and the prices charged for the irreplaceable national resources that are exported. As seldom in the course of history, these processes were highlighted and evaluated during the three years of the Allende presidency.

All of Latin America is consequently affected by the violent counterrevolution which ended the effort to create a just social order in Chile within the framework of constitutional legality. Chile had enjoyed longer periods of civic peace under democratic and constitutional governments than most of its neighbors, and it had treasured its traditional commitment to constitutional processes. But when these processes threatened the monopoly of power of the oligarchs, the sectional interests outweighed the vaunted commitments and traditions. If that happened in Chile, other Latin Americans are forced to ask what prospect *they* have to bring about the necessary changes other than violence.

That rapid and radical change is essential for all of Latin America is no longer an issue. The facts are all too visible. Even Nelson Rockefeller's 1969 report to President Nixon records the basic point. "The gap between the advantaged and the disadvantaged, within nations as well as between nations, is ever sharper and ever more difficult to endure." This is indeed the primary point. While a small proportion of Latin Americans, perhaps five percent, live in extreme luxury, and a further 20 to 25 percent live reasonably, the absolute majority of all Latin Americans live at a level which does not give them enough food, clothing and shelter to meet minimum human requirements. This underprivileged group is growing both in absolute numbers and relative to the entire population. If things continue the way they are going, it will within a single generation have become an albatross around the neck not only of Latin America but of the world.

There is agreement on the need to change this situation. But there is basic disagreement about the way to do it. On the one side are those who claim that our present system of private enterprise, spurred by the urge for endless gain known as the profit motive, can resolve all problems. By giving adequate encouragement to the enormous companies with headquarters in the United States, allowing them to operate freely in the poor countries to the south, to fix the direction and rate of growth, and to determine their own share of the results in the form of profits, the entire hemisphere could gradually be transformed and reach the level of well-being already enjoyed by the majority of North Americans and a quarter of Latin Americans.

Those who make this claim are fewer in number each year. But they are still enormously powerful through their accumulation in a small interlocking network of most of the resources not only of the United States but of the world. The president and administration of the United States identify with them and their objectives. They control the media of information in the United States and in most of the world outside the Soviet and China orbits. Through these various power elements and structures they still command the support of vast numbers of people.

4

Here we are faced with a paradox, one which the Allende experience has helped to sharpen. The power of these supporters of the status quo grows each year. They are expanding their monopoly of world resources at an incredible rate. They are developing new techniques of control, more efficient weapons of destruction with which to impose their will by brute force when necessary, more sophisticated techniques of surveillance, interrogation and thought control to render the use of force progressively less necessary. Yet their base is constantly being eroded as more of the politicized and educated strata of society reject their views and withdraw their moral support.

This withdrawal of legitimation from the supporters of the status quo must be seen in the context of Chilean history, of the history of Chile as part of a Latin America which has for centuries been a dependent subsystem of a broader economic and political system, and also in the context of a worldwide thrust to lift the human race to a more human living style and level.

As recently as a quarter century ago, Chile still looked on itself as different from other Latin American countries. During the centuries of Spanish control, it had indeed a significantly different experience. It had few of the precious metals which mesmerized the Spaniards. In consequence, they paid little attention to it, allowing it to become a basically self-sufficient agricultural community. The soil and climate were excellent. The population was sparse, fewer than half a million when the country became independent with an area six times that of New York State. This meant living space and work for everyone, and in consequence low social pressures. By the same methods as in the United States and in Argentina, the Indians had been exterminated or isolated in the inhospitable southern regions, with the result that the population was far more homogeneous than that of the neighboring Andean countries. Ignored by Spain's entrepreneurs and tax gatherers, it

5

was able to accumulate slowly its own capital in the form not only of buildings but of education, so that by the nineteenth century it was ahead of most Latin American countries in intellectual and cultural life. In one fundamental respect, nevertheless, Chile was like all other Latin American societies from the outset. It was a society divided rigidly by class. The Spaniards have made many contributions to human development, but they have always lagged in their understanding of human rights. For them, the structure of human relations is dominated by the Roman concept of the paterfamilias who alone is the repository of the rights of all who depend on him. He has obligations indeed, but they derive from his status and function, not from the rights of those toward whom he exercises obligations. In Chile, as elsewhere, the *patrón* became the paterfamilias. He alone owned land, vast extensions of it, and he determined who might use part of what he owned, and under what conditions. The ownership of land, restricted to a handful of the king's favorites in the first instance and regulated ever since by their successors as a self-perpetuating group, determined class and rights. All other Chileans were classless and rightless. From the outset, the twin pillars of Latin American society, the church and the army, served the patrón in maintaining this order. The priest conditioned the rural worker into accepting his place, telling him he was favored by God here on earth in having so generous a patrón, and was assured of even greater favors hereafter as his reward for serving this patrón faithfully. This contributed to the creation of a docile rural labor force, apolitical, respectful, voting the way the patrón told them. One of several significant changes in the immediate past (as will be explored later) is the partial withdrawal of the church from this function of legitimating the class structure.

While society was basically rural and uncrowded, the priest was normally able to maintain the social order

6

without the help of more force than what the patrón could provide from his own resources. But even then the army was involved in constant hostilities with the Indians, and in some areas the distinction of race and culture between Indians and settled peasants was slight. And from the middle of the nineteenth century, with the development of mining and the building of harbors and other facilities to handle the minerals, a new type of worker developed who often required major force to keep him in his place. One of the most widespread myths about Chile is that its armed forces are apolitical. Apart from the intrinsic absurdity of the idea that any institution of a nation can be apolitical, the history of Chile establishes quite clearly the political function of the armed forces in maintaining the monopoly of power of the ruling class. Specifics will be found in the next chapter.

The big change in Chile's situation, the one that has gradually brought it ever more fully into the same politico-economic condition as other Latin Americans, began in the second quarter of the nineteenth century when Britain replaced Spain as its trading partner. Unlike the Spaniards, the British quickly found resources to exploit in the form of nitrates for the control of which Chile fought a war with Bolivia and Peru. With rising populations, rising living standards and imperialistic ambitions, Europe had an insatiable appetite for fertilizers and explosives. Thus was begun the distortion of the Chilean economy to serve the needs and benefits of the foreign companies which quickly ousted the Chilean mine operators. Soon American copper interests joined the British nitrate miners, expanding to their longtime domination of the Chilean economy when the demand for nitrates fell as a result of Germany's development of synthetic substitutes.

The profits from mining were such that the foreign companies could afford to pay the administrative costs of government. In return, the oligarchy ensured wage levels and work conditions to their liking, with the army on hand when necessary to keep the workers in place. Commerce and banking were geared to their specific needs, and public works were concentrated on transport, port and other facilities they used. They encouraged stagnancy in all other sectors of the economy, not only because this kept the wages they had to pay relatively low, but because they always feared that a strong Chile would assert ownership rights. In particular, they resisted successfully every attempt to force them to process the minerals in Chile, in part because they sought to give the home country the benefit of the more sophisticated and profitable part of the operation, in part because they would be more vulnerable to expropriation. To keep food prices for their workers and other urban labor low, they supported a system of food price controls which discouraged investment in agriculture. The long-term effect, as population grew, was to divert profits from mining export to the purchase of food for importation. This had a double benefit for the foreign companies. Ships arriving for ore carried profitable cargoes of foodstuffs from their homeland. Chile's permanent stagnation and dependency were assured, since the capital that might have enabled it to develop its agriculture and industry was effortlessly dissipated. The development of import-substitution industires in the 1930s further impoverished agriculture.

Even in colonial times, the ruling class had needed a wide range of skilled services, clergy, lawyers, teachers and artisans. The range of needs and the numbers involved grew substantially as the country adapted itself to a mining economy, with banks, accountants, salesmen and all the paraphernalia of the modern city and the consumer society. To call this a middle class and to interpret it as a dynamic force leading the country toward modernity is to misunderstand its origin and function. The middle classes are a phenomenon of the industrial society which developed in Western Europe and the United States and which did indeed perform important functions in bringing them to the kind of material development these areas enjoy. The service class in Chile and similar countries, sometimes called the middle sector, lacks social cohesion or clear self-identification. Its dependence on the upper class is such as often to force it to adopt short-term policies clearly in conflict with its longer-term interests.

The establishment of a political system based on the theories of the French Revolution in the republics established when Latin America broke away from Spain was not intended to change the basic assumptions on which the society functioned. The decisions were still to be made by the ruling class, and the dependent middle sectors were to intervene merely in their role of servants. As for the rest of society, it was never imagined that the workers and peasants, the *peones*, would participate in decision-making. Their sole political function was to assemble on polling day to vote their patrón's line. For this he handed them a suitably colored piece of paper, to make checking the easier.

The development of mining brought the first change in this psychology of dependence and resignation. From 1850 to 1880 Chile was already the first producer of copper in the world. The lure of high wages drew workers from the farms to the mining camps. But life there was rough and expensive. Safety regulations were non-existent, as were benefits for the injured or pensions for those too old to work. By the 1870s, long before their counterparts in other Latin American countries were politically conscious, the miners, dockers and other city workers were asking to be enfranchised. That meant that they had begun to develop a class consciousness, an awareness of their powerlessness in their dealings with a system controlled by their employers. Their numbers and sense of class identification grew rapidly with a boom in nitrates which brought

large numbers of workers from the central valley to Antofagasta and Iquique in the north. By 1886, the demands
of the workers for recognition had become so audible that
a liberal president, José Manuel Balmaceda, came to power
with a commitment to give them some voice in the political process. But the conservative majority in Congress
would have none of it and plunged the country into the
most serious civil war in its history. Balmaceda was defeated and committed suicide. The following years saw the
first strikes, beginning in the north of the country and
gradually spreading southward. This new militancy of the
workers was stimulated and fed by a wave of emigration
from Europe. Thirty thousand workers, most of them
skilled, came from Italy and Spain between 1895 and
1912. They brought with them a tradition of class identity
and a conviction that the only concessions granted by
employers were those won by force. It was at this period
that the labor movement in Chile assumed the syndicalist
and anarchist orientation and ideology which long dominated it. No labor legislation had yet been enacted, and
organization of workers had to be conducted in strictest
secrecy and at the peril of those involved. In spite of
restrictions and pressures, leaders were found to organize
strike and even establish labor newspapers. In the prosperity brought about by the First World War and the opening
of the Panama Canal, the Congress threw a few crumbs of
social legislation to selected workers in the form of acci-
dent compensation and railroad workers' retirement. But
the worker's share in prosperity remained minimal. As Luis
Emilio Recabarren said on the occasion of the first centen-
nial of the republic in 1918, "in all this progress from
which the country has benefited, the proletariat has not
received anything except by contributing to it for the
enjoyment of our adversaries."

The first legal organization of workers began in 1909 as
a "tame" mutual aid society inspired by conservative prin-

10

ciples. This Chilean Workers' Federation (FOCH) was gradually transformed into a militant organization, serving as a focus for nearly 300 strikes between 1911 and 1920. In 1912 Recabarren founded the first working-class political party, the Socialist Workers' Party, which ten years later changed its name to the Communist Party of Chile and joined the Third International, the coordinating body of national communist parties established in Moscow in 1919. Recabarren was then also head of FOCH and he affiliated it with the Communist International Trade Union Movement, also headquartered in Moscow. In 1931, the Communist Party was officially recognized, meaning that it was authorized to present candidates for national and local elections.

The convulsions of the Great Depression brought into existence yet another voice for the have-nots, the Socialist Party founded in 1933. It shared with the Communist Party a marxist ideology, and it worked closely with the Communist Party, apart from occasional clashes. But it identified directly with the situation of the workers in Chile, refusing to adjust to the changing Moscow line. It stressed the class war more than did the Communist Party, tending in the 1960s to sympathize with Castro and Mao. Salvador Allende, one of the Socialist Party founders, was its presidential candidate in 1952. He received only 5.4 percent of the vote. By 1958 he had so strengthened his position that, as head of a coalition of opposition parties, he lost to the candidate of the ruling class, Jorge Alessandri, by a mere 35,000 votes.

The extraordinary showing of the workers' coalition shocked the ruling class and the subordinate middle sectors identified with it. Even if the rural masses were still dependable, the rapid growth of the urban centers, including the slums that mushroomed around them (*callampas*), was creating a situation in which the traditional methods of control were outmoded. As a measure that would serve at least as a stop-gap, the franchise was extended to illiterates. It had a few years earlier been granted to women who, with their tradition of respect for church authority, could be counted on to vote against a marxist, even when their husbands supported him. The illiterate vote would be mostly rural and thus similarly amenable to the instructions of the priest and the patrón.

Meanwhile, powerful interests looked to the rising Christian Democrats as a bulwark against the extreme left. The origins of this party went back to 1937 when Eduardo Frei and other young Catholic intellectuals founded the Falange Nacional, a name obviously inspired by the Falangist Party of fascist tendencies which was at that time helping Franco to power in Spain's civil war. When Christian Democrat parties developed in several countries of Western Europe after the Second World War, the Falange Nacional adopted their name and policies. In Chile they thought of themselves as being slightly left of center but to the right of the Communist Party and the Socialist Party. They spoke at first of a "communitarian society" which would eliminate private control of the means of production (though not necessarily the private ownership) and would allow the state to plan the economy, determine goals and allocate priorities. By 1967, some members were talking about a noncapitalist way of development, and the Christian Democrat presidential candidate in 1970, Radomiro Tomic, promised that if elected he would "dismantle capitalism." About this time, the word *socialism* crept cautiously into the Christian Democrat vocabulary, but usually labeled—to avoid offence to Catholic supporters— as modified or nonmarxist socialism. But the dominant and operative characteristic of Christian Democracy was its commitment to the theory of developmentalism as sponsored by the United Nations and enshrined in the Alliance for Progress. While recognizing that the poor countries had not progressed very far since this approach was proposed in the late 1940s, they insisted that a government truly dedicated to the interests of all the people—not merely those of the upper class—could make it work by channeling the energies and resources of the country into types of economic production that would benefit not only the rich but also the poor.

Thanks to the extreme right, heavy subsidization by the government and transnational companies of the United States, and the votes of a substantial majority of women, Frei won the presidential elections of 1964 with 56.1 percent of the vote to 38.9 percent for Allende. In power, the Christian Democrats soon fell short of their promise. At the end of six years, the gap between rich and poor had not narrowed, and the economy was not significantly more dynamic in spite of a massive input of foreign aid and a corresponding increase in the country's indebtedness. But significant changes had occurred during the Frei administration. A workable land reform law had been passed and a start had been made on implementation. More important, laws which had previously prevented more than token trade unionism of rural labor had been eliminated and massive organization of rural workers and small farmers had immediately followed. The techniques used by the Christian Democrats to enlist a mass following had drawn great numbers of both rural and urban workers to the center of a political process in which they had previously been marginal, a change which quickly redounded to the benefit of the extreme left and permanently enlarged its power base. The process also affected the Christian Democrat party itself. As worker tensions resulting from unfulfilled expectations increased, Frei found himself more and more dependent on the right. In an attempt to curb inflation, the government proposed in 1967 a cut in worker salaries and a temporary ban on strikes. A nationwide protest strike was called, and the government responded with massive force. In Santiago, United States trained and

13

supplied soldiers and the Grupo Móvil (specially trained anti-riot police) used helicopters, tear gas, crowd-control tanks, and guns. Seven were killed, four of them children. Some time later, the Grupo Móvil was assigned to evict a hundred farmworker families who had peacefully occupied unused land at Puerto Montt. They killed nine people and injured thirty in the operation. This rightist trend caused a split in the Christian Democrats. In May 1969, a group led by Jacques Chonchol formed the Movement of United Popular Action (MAPU). And as the elections approached, Radomiro Tomic found it necessary as the party's presidential candidate to formulate a program far to the left of the policies followed by Frei as president.

In addition to drawing considerable numbers of previously nonpoliticized rural workers into the political process, the Christian Democrats furthered the process by forcing a previously monolithic church to opt for political pluralism. For large and important sectors of the population, this made little difference. Industrial and mining workers, scientists and professional men, university professors and politicians had for the most part long been alienated from the church.[2] But church influence remained strong among women of all classes, and also to some extent among rural men. The party of the oligarchs, the National Party, could count on votes from these groups for as long as the church retained its traditional identification with it. For that reason, its response was violent when in the 1950s the Christian Democrats claimed for themselves the mantle of religion and promised to remake Chile in the social and economic blueprint set out in papal social teachings from Pope Leo XIII to Pope Pius XI. It had enjoyed a powerful mouthpiece in the theological magazine *Mensaje*. Gradually, their views prevailed, so that by the 1960s more Catholics thought of the Christian Democrats than of the National Party as representing their institutional concerns. But what was more important, the monolithic image was smashed. Catholics had to make a political judgment on the merits, and as class consciousness grew, this inevitably worked in favor of the parties of the left.

There still remained, nevertheless, the bogy of marxism. A constant of all the papal social teachings, more stressed than their strictures on the capitalist system, was their absolute condemnation of everything associated with Karl Marx, and nowhere in the world did the bishops have this preoccupation more on their minds than in Latin America. The first hemispheric meeting ever of the bishops of Latin America was held at Rio de Janeiro in 1955. They concluded that a shortage of priests was their biggest problem, and that their most urgent task was to fight Protestantism, Communism, Spiritism and Free Masonry, with the communists the most dangerous of all their adversaries.

Within a decade, nevertheless, priorities were to be drastically revised. The Second Vatican Council from 1962 to 1965 revealed a hitherto little suspected concern among bishops around the world with the social problem. Archbishop Helder Camara of Recife, Brazil, Bishop Manuel Larraín of Talca, and Bishop Sergio Méndez Arceo of Cuernavaca, Mexico, were among the church leaders who emerged as committing the church to a new relationship with the suffering masses of humanity, a program which quickly identified them as on a collision course with the status quo. The logic of the new commitment became clearer when at the end of 1965 the Colombian priest-sociologist Camilo Torres joined a guerrilla band and gave his life in a gesture of violent disassociation from his society. Many church spokesmen disapproved, yet ever since Camilo has been an inspiration to priests and people. Soon, groups of progressive priests and lay people committed to his ideals were forming everywhere, Golconda in Colombia, Onis in Peru, Iglesia Joven in Chile, the Third World Movement in Argentina.

The extent of the change of attitude was revealed at Medellín, Colombia, in September 1968. A meeting of the bishops of all Latin America, which Pope Paul had opened when he visited Bogotá the previous month, came out with a Message to the Peoples of Latin America which was a death knell of an old order and a call for volunteers to build a new one. The bishops rejected the long-held notion that God was on the side of the powerful. On the contrary, they said, he sent his son "to free all men from all forms of slavery in which they are held by sin, ignorance, hunger, misery and oppression." Using more openly marxist language than had ever before appeared in an official statement from responsible church leaders, they denounced the oppressing power used by institutions to impose violence, the neocolonialism of the national oligarchies, and the external neocolonialism of "the international monopolies and the international imperialism of money," on which the system rested. They noted and rejected explicitly the "justifications"—such as the threat of communism and the need to maintain order—offered by the guardians of the status quo for the use of force against people who try to promote change. They listed specifically the growing distortion of international commerce caused by decline of raw material prices while those of manufactured goods rose, the flight of capital, the brain drain, the tax evasions, and the export of profits and dividends by foreign companies "without contributing adequate reinvestments to the progressive development of our countries," the growing burden of debt. All of this, they said, is imperialism exercised over Latin America not only in indirect ways but even by direct interventions.

"Many parts of Latin America are experiencing a situation of injustice which can be called institutionalized violence. The structures of industry and agriculture, of the national and the international economy, the cultural and political life all violate fundamental rights. Entire peoples

16

lack the bare necessities and live in a condition of such dependency that they can exercise neither initiative or responsibility. Similarly, they lack all possibility of cultural improvement and of participation in social and political life. Such situations call for global, daring, urgent, and basically renewing change. It should surprise nobody that the temptation to violence should manifest itself in Latin America. It is wrong to abuse the patience of people who have endured for years a situation that would be intolerable if they were more aware of their rights as human beings."[3]

Not all Catholics by any means listened to this call. Many continued to attribute to the church its traditional role as supporter of the powerful, preaching resignation to the poor in their poverty and threatening hellfire on those who would resist the commands of constituted authority, including that of the *patrón* whom God had placed over them and given power over them. But the former unanimity within the church was gone forever. The most dynamic and informed elements switched allegiance. The same change occurred among Protestants whose influence in Latin America is often far greater than their relatively small numbers. Indeed the polarization among Protestants has been even greater than that among Roman Catholics. Many young Protestant intellectuals have for some considerable time been discussing among themselves the need for institutional change as a preliminary to any meaningful Christianization of the masses. They were greatly encouraged by the spread of similar ideas among progressive Catholics during and after the Vatican Council, and the two movements quickly established a firm liaison. But when they reached the point of identifying not only the local oligarchs but also the United States as involved in the oppression of the poor, those progressive Protestants found themselves in open conflict with the governing bodies of their churches, bodies composed largely of men

17

identified by education and business interest with the United States. The main expression of this progressive movement among Protestants is a hemispheric organization known as ISAL, acronym for *Iglesia y Sociedad en América Latina* (Church and Society in Latin America). Through ISAL they work in full harmony and understanding with the progressive elements in the Catholic church, to the amazement of all who remember the gulf that still existed in 1955.

All of this represented an enormous broadening of the options open to the Catholic. It was possible to accept the new theory of dependence which represented the poor countries as not only the historical but the continuing victims of the avarice and power of the rich countries, an extension of the concept of class warfare to the international sphere. Such was clearly the analysis of the bishops at Medellín. Some Catholics were beginning to say that one could go farther and accept the entirety of the marxist analysis of the distortions of the capitalist system, including the concept of class warfare, without subscribing to the errors—particularly the atheism—of Marx's philosophy. Few, however, were prepared in the 1960s to go so far. It was not until 1971 that a papal document admitted for the first time, grudgingly and with a series of reservations, the possibility that a Christian might use the marxist social analysis.[4] Instead, a nonmarxist theory of revolution, of Christian socialism, was sought. This attempt has had and continues to have an important—usually divisive—influence on the revolutionary movement in Latin America. It is absolutely necessary to understand it in order to clarify the forces which operated to bring Allende to power, which affected his policy while president, and which continue to bear on the future of the revolution in Chile.

The socialism proposed by the Christian Democrats in their platform for the 1970 election was nonmarxist, rejecting the need for class consciousness and class struggle.

It presented the people of all classes and categories, or at least all with the exception of the oligarchs who had formally allied themselves with the external oppressors, as capable of being brought together in a society in which power and decision-making would be decentralized and democratized by cooperative control of production. In practice this policy pushed the party into arrangements with conservatives and caused internal conflict. MAPU had already broken with the Christian Democrats on the issue of class struggle. As Frei moved to the right in opposition after 1970, bringing most of the party with him, a more radical wing moved in the direction MAPU had taken and finally left the party structures. The internal polarization has become still more acute following the military seizure of power.

Within the marxist ranks, in Chile and elsewhere, important ideological differences also existed. Orthodox marxist theory looks to the workers alone as the makers of the revolution, and principally to the organized industrial workers as developed in the capitalist homelands on whose experience Marx based his theory. In countries like Chile, it looks to the concentration of power, including ownership and control of the means of production, in the hands of the state as a step toward the ultimate objective of worker control. Orthodox communist parties, such as the Communist Party of Chile, have in consequence consistently supported bourgeois revolutions, like Peronism in Argentina today or the nationalist military regime in Peru, and some marxist theoreticians suggest that the support is not merely tactical but results from a convergence of ideology. Since such programs, while threatening to the oligarchs, tend to benefit the middle sectors of society, they can be made acceptable to pragmatic parties with little ideological content like Chile's Radical Party.

Other marxists, starting from sociological situations very different from that of Marx, as in China and Cuba, find the need to identify the class struggle differently. For them, the whole oppressed people is the subject of the struggle against the alliance of internal and external oppressors, and indeed the organized workers, as a relatively privileged group created and maintained by foreign capitalist interests, can even range itself on the side of conservatism. These theories in their extreme form reject the values of the capitalist world and seek to create a world without money or other material inducements, a world built on a new kind of man, the "new man" first envisaged by St. Paul, whose values exclude selfishness and upgrade social goals. In this society, work would be voluntary. Rewards would be equal for all. The workers would control the enterprise in which they work. Justice would be done in people's courts. The revolution would be made by those who make it, not by a "party," and all are to be welcomed regardless of class, beliefs or party allegiance. The stress is on activism and charisma, and while in theory the dynamism comes from within the people, in Chile the leaders were mostly intellectuals who had established themselves in city slums and in peasant villages. But even if leadership was from outside, it did not mean the manipulation from outside of inert populations, as in the past. As will be seen, a remarkable development of energies and social awareness quickly occurred.

Such nonmarxist leftists as MAPU and MIC, even if theoretically to the right of both groups of marxists, found themselves emotionally more in tune with the extremists identified with Cuba and China, than with the rigidly structured program of the orthodox, Moscow-oriented variant. All these elements functioned within the Allende coalition, the orthodox marxists always seeking a concentration of power and productive capacity in the state but with the least possible damage to the existing system, the others subordinating economics to the imperative of mobilization of the masses and political transformation.

20

Chile, accordingly, had in 1970 organized political parties covering the spectrum from the extreme right to the extreme left, each representing a segment of conscious opinion. The viewpoint each party represented clearly reflected in some instances the class interests of those who shared it. In other instances it was less than fully representative of those interests, because of ideological presuppositions or of historical conditionings. The major parties, starting from the right, were these.

National Party. A fusion of the traditional Conservative and Liberal parties (which, as generally in Latin America, had represented the landowning and commercial wings of the oligarchy respectively), it is the unequivocal voice of the oligarchy. Its voting strength is among urban professionals and businessmen, middle-class women, and peasants who follow the dictates of their landlord employers. Its voting power in Congress is increased by a rural bias in the drawing of constituencies.

Christian Democrats. Started in 1937 by young Catholic intellectuals looking for an alternative to the conservatism of the National Party, it adopted a moderate left position in the 1950s, seeking social progress and a fairer distribution of the national income through development of existing economic structures, later moved cautiously toward nonmarxist socialism stressing cooperative ownership of the means of production. Leadership derived from Catholic intellectual circles, with support of elements in the clergy. Popular base in urban middle sectors, also among peasants wooed away from previous support of National Party.

Radical Party. Formed in 1862 as a reaction against oligarchic rule, it has represented the center in Chilean politics since the early 1930s, deriving its support from small businessmen and civil servants. Pragmatic and with "anticlerical" liberalism as its historic base, it led a "Popular Front" coalition with the Communist Party, and several smaller parties, which won the presidential elections in 1938 and held power for several years. It supported Jorge Alessandri in 1958, Eduardo Frei in 1964, and Salvador Allende in 1970.

MAPU. The Movement of United Popular Action resulted from the defection of the left wing of the Christian Democrats in 1969 in protest against the rightward drift of the party when in power. Stands for a more aggressive implementation of Christian Democrat policies, with acceptance of the class struggle as an historical fact.

Communist Party. Formed as the Chilean Socialist Workers' Party in 1912, it changed its name and joined Moscow's Third International in 1922, from which time it has generally followed Moscow's line. Party membership in the late 1960s was estimated at about 50,000, higher than that of any other Latin American country except Cuba. Support came mainly from organized labor and other elements of the urban proletariat. Relative conservative and legalistic in its promotion of revolutionary policies.

Socialist Party. Founded in 1933 to present marxist policies in independence of Moscow, it has generally been farther to the left than the Communist Party with which its relations have varied from cool to cordial, and with which it has formed various coalitions. Leadership largely from intellectuals and university students, and popular base primarily among organized workers and people in the urban slums.

MIR. The Movement of the Revolutionary Left was formed from several splinter groups at the University of Concepción in 1965. It stood for militant class struggle, insisting that the haves would use all force at their disposal before yielding power, and that consequently the have-nots must arm for the inevitable conflict. Encouraged direct action by local groups, using violence as needed, to seize land and other resources. Strong among homeless squatters of Santiago and of some rural areas, never a big

22

party but exercising great influence through its forceful methods and high esprit de corps.

To understand the interplay between these political parties, and the voter basis sought by each, requires some analysis of the classes and subgroups who make up the society. In Latin America, in general, one can distinguish a ruling class containing about five percent of the population. It lives at a level equal to or higher than that of the wealthiest people in industrially developed countries. Next come middle classes or sectors, about 15 to 20 percent of the population, embracing a spectrum which runs from lawyers and doctors at one end to store assistants and other white-collar workers at the other. Their life style is similar to that of the middle classes in industrially developed countries. Below them come unskilled workers, some 40 percent of the total, whose income allows them to live just above the starvation level, with minimum quantity and quality of food, clothing and shelter. Below them again is an equal number of marginal people, surplus to the needs of the economy, unemployed or engaged in unproductive activities, suffering from malnutrition and other deficiencies which lead to unemployability and early death. Members of these two lower groups, especially the bottom one, tend to be marked by a psychology of dependence and fatalism.

Chile is typical of Latin America in having a five percent upper class, but its middle class is well above average at 30 percent. The marginals are probably less than half of the lower class. Since only a quarter of the population is now rural, most of the marginals are found in the shantytowns surrounding the cities. The rural lower class is itself divided into many subgroups, some with significantly distinct values and expectations. They include permanent salaried workers, sharecroppers, owners of very small farms and migrant workers. In a total peasant population of 2.5 million, small farmers number more than 280,000, and about half of the 700,000 agricultural workers are salaried. It is only in the past decade that the peasantry has emerged as a social force in Chile. Before that, the class struggle was conducted almost entirely by the urban and mining workers. Rural trade unions were absolutely forbidden by law until 1947, and restrictions in force until the Christian Democrats came to power in 1964 held them to a nominal level. By 1970, the rural union strength, mostly among permanent salaried workers was 140,000, with two thirds of the members in unions controlled by or sympathetic to the Christian Democrats. After the UP government came to power, the rural unions grew substantially in strength, and the number of members of unions backing the UP program rose to about half the total. Small farmers, some of them organized in a union, tended to identify with the Christian Democrats or with the National Party, the traditional political affiliation of the countryside. Cooperativists, many of them beneficiaries of the expanded land reform of the UP government, favored leftist trade unions supporting the UP. Many of the non-organized peasants—the great majority—remained politically uninvolved and voted the traditional National Party line. Others, however, were greatly influenced in some areas by the peasant section of MIR and were mobilized into peasant associations which developed their own internal dynamism and engaged in land seizures and other direct actions calculated to change the balance of power and control of wealth in the countryside.

The oligarchy is the group in Chile which has the greatest consciousness of its group identity and interests. In line with its awareness of its minority character, it has traditionally sought to minimize class identification and to represent itself as the selfless and natural moderator of the interests of all sectors. With the growth of the strength and self-understanding of other groups, it has used its resources—particularly its near monopoly of the media of

24

communications—to woo the allegiance of some sectors by favoring them over others, and to promote conflict and division among those who most threatened. It stressed law and order while these protected it, but—as will appear—when they ceased to be on its side, it did not hesitate to step outside them.

The middle sectors, as defined by income, education, professional standing and urban outlook, cover a wide range of attitudes and interests. The civil servants, for example, have little in common with the 50,000 owner-drivers of trucks. They tend to be socially cohesive, however, going to the same schools, clubs and beaches, reading the same books, and watching the same movies and television programs, all of which keeps a gulf between them and the inhabitants of the *poblaciones* (slums) which ring the cities in which they live. Their political allegiance is widely distributed. They are the main support of the Christian Democrats. But significant minorities favor parties of the Left. In the polarization that marked the last year of the Allende government, most of the teachers in public schools backed the government, as did the very important national health service. It was also supported by nearly all the artists, writers and other intellectuals, a group in which Chile is particularly rich, and by 20 to 25 percent of doctors, dentists, architects and engineers.

Organized labor constituted the spearhead of the drive for better conditions for the oppressed masses from the very start of the movement, and it was still the most clearly identifiable element of support for the Communist Party and the Socialist Party. But even organized labor was far from homogeneous in its attitudes. As in Latin America generally, white-collar workers and blue-collar workers are organized in separate unions, and in many mines and industries in which the Left controlled the blue-collar workers, the Christian Democrats controlled the others. This influenced voting patterns at election times, but in the polarization of the summer of 1973, especially in the defense of the factories by workers after the abortive tank revolt in June, many Christian Democrat unions rejected their party's lead and joined the workers of the Left.

The *poblaciones* which mushroomed around Santiago and the other cities in the 1950s and 1960s introduced a new element into the struggle. Most of their inhabitants were unemployed or engaged in casual, shifting work, and in consequence were not unionized. At the same time, these people were far from being the *rotos* (broken ones) as they were derisively called by the well-to-do. They are the most dynamic and enterprising of the rural population, people who have the initiative to strike out into the unknown in search of a better life. As this fact was recognized during the 1960s, it led to major efforts of community development and politicization by parties ranging from the Christian Democrats in the left-center to MIR on the extreme left. The Socialist Party also participated enthusiastically, but the Communist Party with less enthusiasm. Its tradition of direction from above made it suspicious of grassroots movements which easily got out of hand. The success of the others, however, forced the Communist Party to go along in order not to be left out in the cold. Soon many of the *poblaciones* created highly developed internal organizations. They formed their own volunteer police forces, or militia as they called them. Camp leaders administered justice. Fighting, wife-beating, drunkenness, games of chance and stealing were prohibited, the penalty for a first offense being a public reprimand, then expulsion from the camp for repeaters. The oligarchs correctly saw the development of a political sense among the *rotos* as the writing on the wall for them. Even before Allende came to power, *El Mercurio* was denouncing "this seed of a vast revolutionary movement based on the formation of irregular units." The *poblaciones* were the first to experience the terror unleashed in Chile after

26

the revolt of the generals in September 1963.
The rural poor were the last to become involved. The
Chilean peasant has been historically passive, untouched
by the messianic and millenary movements which have
flourished in Brazil's Northeast, or by the social banditry
endemic in Colombia. He is marked by a psychology of
dependence and fatalism, involved in personal rather than
institutional relationships. He has difficulty in seeing the
structural nature of his poverty, or in believing he can do
anything about it. His values, world-view and self-concept
are not made by him but "received" from his patrón.[5] It
was only during the 1960s that this situation changed
significantly, largely as a result of broader social change in
Chile which produced the movement for land reform and
drove the political parties to the countryside in search of
votes. Up to that time, the peasant had followed the
guidance of his patrón, reinforced by the priest, and voted
for the reactionary National Party. The Christian Democrats, as the party in power when the land reform began,
were the first beneficiaries. But in the extreme south,
where poverty was greatest and the control of the landlords most absolute, the organization of the peasants was
prevented until the UP government came to power in
1970. Then the late-developing peasant consciousness responded to the most advanced revolutionary ideas,
methods of struggle and organization. Encouraged by MIR,
the people organized rural collectives and took possession
of land without concern for legal details.

Although the poorest groups in Chile, as represented by
the slum dwellers and the peasants, are the last to join
actively in community building and recognition of group
interests, sociologist James Petras has noted that their
degree of participation and their interest in participating
and in making decisions is far higher than that of the other
groups who were involved before them. In an extensive
study he found the highest degree of interest in participa-

tion, interaction and solidarity among the squatters of the Santiago poblacion, called New Havana (a name changed by the generals to Village of Flowers). Next came the peasants belonging to Socialist and MIR peasant unions in the provinces of Nuble and Cautín. The textile workers from Hirmas followed, then the miners of El Teniente, and in last place the miners of Chuquicamata. He ascribes the lower class consciousness of the copper workers in part to their geographic isolation, in part to their "sectoral economic consciousness" as members of a privileged labor group, in part to exposure to the United States view that trade unionism should deal with economic issues to the exclusion of the political. The squatters and the peasants, by contrast, had little prior schooling in electoral or union politics. They came direct to the action of seizure of their property, an action frequently organized from below and carried out by the people themselves. They were thus faced immediately with the bigger questions of management and administration.[6]

The development of these various groups, attitudes and strategies will be presented in more detail in subsequent chapters. It will be seen that the attempt to restructure Chilean society between 1970 and 1973 was not an isolated, fortuitous interlude in the country's life, or the whim of a crazy or inspired individual, but a logical step in the upward thrust of a people. Six parties, each with its own strategic and tactical approach and its commitment to a political base, joined in the UP coalition which carried Allende to power. MIR did not join the coalition but urged its supporters to vote for Allende and undertook to support—with reservations—his efforts to implement his proclaimed objectives. At the same time, it made clear that it did not think he could succeed because he undertook to govern "with the capitalist state apparatus remaining untouched," and it said it would "maintain our political and military structure" until the capitalist system was over-

28

thrown and power effectively controlled by the workers. The National Party maintained an attitude of total opposition and hostility to Allende from the start. The Christian Democrats agreed both before and after the elections to certain tactical arrangements in return for commitments which limited significantly Allende's freedom of action as president. Having won these concessions, the Christian Democrats moved almost immediately to open opposition, providing with the National Party an overwhelming obstacle in Congress to presidential action.

Given this strong opposition and the heterogeneous nature of his coalition, Allende had none of the characteristics of the traditional Latin American caudillo. While he was a charismatic figure with outstanding political ability and played a historic part in catalyzing worker movements in Chile, the meaning of UP's attempt to lead Chile toward socialism by constitutional methods must be sought less in the president than in the social movements on which he depended and within which he had to maneuver. As a corollary, his death did not alter radically the fundamental equations. The circumstances in which it occurred will undoubtedly influence future strategy, but the forces through which he worked are the same today as yesterday.

1.

From
Political Independence
to Economic Dependency

Chileans greeted the twentieth century with euphoric anticipations. This was to be the Chilean century. The armed forces had decisively defeated the combined strength of Bolivia and Peru in the War of the Pacific. The territories ceded to Chile included the Bolivian province of Atacama, renamed Antofagasta. This province, Bolivia's only outlet to the sea, had been the direct cause of the war when Bolivia cancelled contracts under which a Chilean firm was exploiting the nitrate deposits. Permanent access to the precious nitrates was now ensured. Chile, with a population doubled to three millions in fifty years and heavily European in its composition, had once more demonstrated the superiority of the white race. It could look forward to participating for the foreseeable future in the civilization of plenty which was now clearly the birthright of Western Europe and North America.

Chile had in fact much reason in 1900 to regard itself as the leading nation of all South America. Its population was close to that of neighboring Argentina; and as its per capita production was significantly higher than that of the Argentines, its economic power was proportionately greater. Brazil had six times as many people, but per capita production there was so much lower that Brazil had no economic edge. As for Venezuela and Colombia, two other countries which would later grow rapidly in numbers and hemispheric influence, they were then so far behind as not to be worthy of consideration.[1]

The pattern of life and geographic distribution of the population of Chile had long since been established. The total area is just under 300,000 square miles, six times that of New York State, but spread out in a narrow band running north and south more than 2,500 miles from the arid equatorial deserts on the borders of Peru and Bolivia to the southernmost tip of the continent. The population, however, was concentrated in one area in the north-center between the cities of Coquimbo and Concepción. These cities are about 500 miles apart. Santiago, the capital, is practically equidistant from them.

About a third or more of this north-central region is occupied by the high Andes which separate it from Argentina. Another third consists of a coastal range of mountains separated from the high Andes by valleys with soils and climate similar to those of California. The Araucanian Indians had established sedentary agriculture with irrigation in these valleys before the Spaniards came. The Spaniards seized their land and parceled it out, mostly in big estates, to the army officers who used the Indians to cultivate it for them. This system of landholding persisted for several centuries. More than half of the privately owned land in the region was until recently concentrated in 375 holdings, the biggest over 600 square miles and none smaller than 20 square miles.[2]

Already by the year 1900, the colonial economy which in the next seventy years would drain away Chile's wealth and hopes of progress, was well established. The small number of Chileans who then had a voice in their country's decisions were, however, not in the least disturbed. It was working well for them, and they were confident it would work even better when carried to its promised peak.

By the end of Spanish rule in the first quarter of the nineteenth century, Chile was exporting substantial amounts of minerals, principally gold but also silver and copper. After independence, Chilean capital continued this exploitation and also began to develop the nitrate industry. The British moved in as merchants just as soon as the Spaniards had moved out as political overlords. In the first instance, however, they did not engage directly in mining, concentrating instead on the areas of trade and shipping which were their specialty. Soon, Britain was buying and transporting nearly two-thirds of Chile's exports and providing more than a third of its imports.

Copper, an essential element for Britain's metallurgical industry, was from the start the most important item for the British traders. Thanks to the steady supply from Chile, the British foundries began to dominate the world copper market. The trade became so important both for Britain and for Chile that the British traders found they could use a weapon which big firms have been using ever since in international trade. They started to pressure both the London and the Santiago governments to modify the laws for their benefit. When Chilean copper magnates started to establish foundries to smelt some of the copper they mined, the British merchants got the British Parliament to act against a measure which threatened the growth of Britain's own copper foundries. They had enough leverage to persuade the government of Chile to grant a monopoly of the steamboat trade along the coasts of Chile to the Pacific Steam Navigation Company. They were similarly able to exercise British government pressure on Chile to repeal a tax on imported coal which had been imposed to protect Chile's own coal producers.

Apart from the minimal quantities needed to start their

trading activities, the British brought practically no capital into Chile. Instead, they used the resources of Chilean capital, obtaining loans from the banks in Valparaiso and Santiago to spread out into banking, the building of railroads and plants for drinking water, office supplies and real estate. Thanks to their superior access to credit and to technology, they were able to force Chileans out of business and gradually acquire control both of copper mining and nitrates. For a time more than 70 percent of all production and exporting were controlled from London, and the internal economy and the Public Treasury became totally dependent on income from exports. In 1879, the fiscal income-dependency on foreign commerce reached the level of 97 percent of the national budget.

Most of the benefit of all this activity returned to Britain, where it was used to capitalize the industrial revolution that made Britain the world's greatest power. It has been estimated, for example, that more than 60 percent of the value of all Chilean nitrate remained in England. But what was left in Chile was enough to pay the costs of government and to keep the upper five percent of Chileans, the group which monopolized power, on the side of the British companies which ran the country. Chile experienced little of the conflict between the big landlords and the commercial bourgeoisie which characterized politics in most Latin American countries in the nineteenth century and continued in many of them well into the twentieth. Instead, many of the landowners participated in commercial activities while retaining their huge estates. Others formed matrimonial alliances with the merchants and bankers. The fact that real power was exercised by foreign interests undoubtedly aided the process of amalgamation of these two groups, a process which was already so far advanced by the 1850s as to permit a liberal-conservative coalition government, and which would culminate a century later in a definitive fusion of the two parties.

33

Before the development of the internal combustion engine and of the electrical industry, mining was mainly an activity of hand labor. A considerable force of workers was consequently developed for Chile's copper and nitrate exploitation in the second half of the nineteenth century. As everywhere in the early stages of capitalism, it was cruelly exploited, until finally in the 1890s it began to acquire a class consciousness and to express its frustrations and needs in a series of strikes which began in the north of the country and gradually spread southward.

Such methods of asserting the worker's claims were universally regarded in those times as absolutely unacceptable deviant behavior, to be put down with all the force at the command of the public authorities. Indeed, the attitudes of the rulers to worker rights were so negative that Luis Emilio Recabarren, principal founder of the labor movement, was excluded from the Chamber of Deputies although legally elected to represent labor. In 1905, during a demonstration against taxes newly imposed on imported beef, 400 were shot down in Santiago, as were 150 miners protesting company policies in Antofagasta.

Even more shocking was the response in December 1907 to labor demonstrations in the city of Iquique. Ten thousand workers from the British-owned nitrate mines came out in the streets to press their demands for higher salaries, improved safety standards and an end to exploitation in the company stores. Soldiers opened fire on them with machine guns, killing two thousand men, women and children. This incident burned itself deeply into the folk soul of Chile, establishing for the employers the pattern of control of workers which would survive down to the present time, and establishing for the workers the treatment they could expect if they attempted to assert demands without the power to back them up. Time and again throughout the twentieth century, even during the liberal reformist regime of Eduardo Frei's Christian Democrats in the 1960s, the army was called out to shoot down obstreperous workers and peasants. The army, as it demonstrated once more during and after the overthrow of Allende in 1973, always retained the Prussian ruthlessness instilled by the German officers who originally organized it and for many years remained its mentors. But it retained this ruthlessness because that was what the ruling class required of it, and which that class also expressed in the private vigilante-style armies of the big landowners. This was the side of the social relationships which the poor saw and which made them responsive in the late 1960s and the early 1970s to the urgings of MIR and other extreme left groups to arm themselves and seize farms and factories.

As long as the rich monopolized power and used it freely, they were able to maintain and intensify the traditional gap between themselves and the poor, and to establish a pattern of consumption which was not seriously challenged until the Allende regime. The Chilean peasant family even in the 1960s was still living on an annual income of $200 to $300 and the industrial worker only fractionally higher. The consumer society's automobiles, ice boxes and other luxuries were effectively available only to the upper classes and to the middle sectors which served them immediately. The typical member of the upper class, a big landowner, had an annual income of between $50,000 and $200,000. He spent 64 percent of this income on his luxurious way of life, which often called for a private plane and for vacations in the United States or Europe. Savings accounted for 21 percent, but little of this was invested by him in modernizing his land, the state making no effort to see that such investment would be attractive. Instead, he either put his savings as a junior partner in a business dominated by foreign interests, or— more likely—he sent it abroad to a safe haven in Switzerland or the United States. In doing this he was undoubtedly motivated in part by the desire to have an anchor to windward in case political changes might counsel exile, but he was also influenced by the fact that he could not compete at home with the transnational companies which enjoyed superior access to credit and technology. The tax system so favored him that he surrendered only 14 percent in principle and often far less in practice to the state. Corresponding figures for England when this comparison was developed in the 1960s were 30 percent of the income of the wealthy spent to maintain a life style, 27 percent invested in domestic agriculture and industry, and 42 percent paid in taxes.[3]

Although the British got into Chile first after the expulsion of the Spaniards, it was not long until United States businessmen began to follow. They encountered strong obstacles at first, not only from British competitors, but from a Chilean antipathy to the United States for its indifference during Chile's fight for independence, and for the imperialistic assumptions Chileans read into the declaration of the Monroe Doctrine in 1822. The United States share of all foreign transactions in Chile was still only 5 percent in 1880, but the proportion grew gradually to nearly 13 percent by the outbreak of the First World War, a war that would alter the factors radically in favor of the United States. The first United States company to install itself in Chile was W.R. Grace, which had heavy investments in neighboring Peru. It began by the acquisition of office buildings, then nitrate lands, and after that it established its shipping company.

The United States became involved in copper production in Chile in 1904, when the Braden Copper Company was formed. The following year it began to exploit El Teniente, today the world's biggest underground copper mine. Its investment was one million dollars. Five years later, Albert C. Burrage, a Boston entrepreneur, acquired Chuquicamata, the world's largest open-pit copper mine. This was shortly afterwards taken over by Anaconda with an investment of $2.5 million through a subsidiary, the Chile Exploration Company. Anaconda had been orga-nized in 1899 by Rockefeller Standard Oil interests, and it continues to be dominated by two of the Rockefeller family banks, First National City and Chase Manhattan. About the same time, Kennecott took over El Teniente from Braden. Kennecott was originally organized by the Guggenheims who have been active in United States and world mining for generations and who already owned Chile's nitrate industry through the Anglo Lautaro Nitrate Company. They were joined by the Morgan banking group in their program to expand exploitation of Chilean copper. Yet another group of United States financiers, including J.P. Morgan, Henry Clay Frick and Ogden Mills, put to-gether a stake of $10 million in the Cerro Corporation to exploit the Cerro de Pasco mines and become the third large producer of copper in Chile.

These various maneuvers had by 1914 placed the Chile-an copper industry firmly in United States hands. With the outbreak of war in Europe in that year, the opportunity came for the United States to replace British and German interests in other areas of the economy. United States investment, about four-fifths of it direct and the rest portfolio, grew from $1.6 billion in 1914 to $2.4 billion in 1919, $3.7 billion in 1924 and $5.2 billion in 1930. To the control of the copper mines the North American interests added a monopoly in the production of electricity, tele-phone services and railroad operations. They gained a leading position in nitrates, built industrial plants and opened banks. All this expansion of United States owner-ship and control of major areas of Chile's life was not achieved by the importation of capital to pay for it. On the contrary, Chile was exporting vast quantities of capital in the form of the minerals which constituted the founda-tion of this fantastic economic empire. Such was the difference between the cost of production and the ultimate selling price at the far end of the vertically integrated copper industry that the United States companies were simultaneously able to finance their growth in Chile and pay enormous dividends to their owners.

According to a statement of the Chile Copper Corporation in 1971, the four big United States companies who had been exploiting Chile's copper, nitrate and iron resources for 60 years had in that time taken out of Chile wealth to the value of $10.8 billion. "This figure is of tremendous significance for Chile," it commented, "if one compares it with the fact that the gross national product achieved throughout the entire existence of the country, that is, approximately 400 years, amounts to $10.5 billion. The conclusion is clear: in a little over half a century these United States companies took out from our country an amount greater than that created by Chileans in terms of industries, highways, cities, ports, schools, hospitals, trade, etc., during our country's entire history." The inequity of the arrangements for dividing the benefits of the joint exploitation of Chile's copper resources was further demonstrated by studies of copper profits around the world made by the Allende government. They showed that both Anaconda and Kennecott derived a vastly higher level of profit from their Chilean operations than from any of their other operations. Anaconda took 20.18 percent of its profits out of Chile. Its profitability level on a worldwide basis was 7.18 percent, but when Chile was excluded, the level for the other operations fell to 3.49 percent. Kennecott's profitability level was 11.63 percent worldwide, ten percent without Chile, and 34.84 percent for Chile alone. [4]

The extent of Chile's dependence on forces not subject to its control became evident as the Great Depression of 1929 deepened the following years. League of Nations studies concluded that no other nation in the world was affected so radically and brutally. The United States firms fixed the price of copper at eight cents (U.S.) in 1931 and lowered it to 5.5 cents in 1932. The sale of copper and nitrates, on which Chile depended for more than 70 percent of its foreign exchange, fell from more than $27 million in 1929 to about $3.5 million in 1932. In one year, between October 1929 and October 1930, imports fell by 88 percent. The impact of massive unemployment was compounded by drastic wage cuts and steep increases in the cost of food and other essential goods. By this time, however, the self-identity and class solidarity of the industrial and mining workers was well established, thanks to the efforts of Luis Recabarren and later of the still illegal Communist Party. Leaders of the middle classes were happy to enlist their support in a struggle to win a share of power. Chief among these was Arturo Alessandri, son of an immigrant Italian mine worker and father of the right-wing Jorge Alessandri defeated by Allende in 1970. He came to power for the first time in 1920 on a program which called for separation of church and state, establishment of a tax on high incomes, government control of the nitrate industry, welfare benefits for workers, more educational facilities, and votes for women. In a scenario which would subsequently be repeated regularly in Chilean politics, his programs were blocked by a Congress dominated by the oligarchy, and he was forced into exile. He returned in 1925 and succeeded in winning approval in a plebiscite for his major constitutional proposals. But once again he came up against the reality of power. For the oligarchs the popular will was operative so long as it coincided with their own. With the open backing of the armed forces, they compelled him to resign the presidency almost immediately.

For six years Chile was ruled dictatorially by a military man, Colonel Carlos Ibáñez. By 1931, however, the Depression had brought such social unrest that he resigned following street fighting in which professors, students, workers and sailors joined. Nine different governments representing every shade of the political spectrum tried unsuccessfully to make order out of the political chaos of the next 18 months. One called itself socialist, though it made no attempt or even commitment to socialize the means of production. However, it did present an analysis of Chile's problems proved valid by subsequent history. "The administration of credit, the exercise of foreign and internal trade, the control óver salaries and the market have escaped our hands. Foreign enterprises have in their power all the heavy industry of the production of raw materials and a large part of public services. Our privileged classes have lived intoxicated with the luxuries and the soft life provided by foreign capitalism in exchange for our natural resources and for the misery of the people."

The armed forces had been the effective rulers of Chile during the previous six years, identifying their interests at all times with those of the oligarchy. They quickly grew tired of the tentative liberal reforms proposed by the new regime, and a new military coup put an end to the Socialist Republic after just a hundred days in power. Among those jailed as troublemakers after the coup was a 23-year-old university student named Salvador Allende, son of a provincial lawyer who served a term in Congress as a deputy for the Radical Party and who was Serene Grand Master of Free Masons in Chile. Shortly after his release Salvador qualified as a doctor but his continued activities in leftist politics, which included the founding in 1933 of the Socialist Party of Chile, effectively excluded him from various jobs he sought. He finally won a foothold in his profession as a dissector of corpses in a hospital, and he later said that his 18 months of post-mortem analyses was the most important training of his life. There he saw vividly the difference between the small number of Chileans who could afford proper medical attention and good food and the vast majority who were undernourished and dependent on the inadequate public medical facilities. A short, stocky man, whose gray hair, neatly trimmed mustache and thick-rimmed glasses in later life gave him a studious appearance, Allende was a born politician. He was an impressive speaker who explained complex economic issues in simple terms. Married and father of three daughters, he dressed well and enjoyed the social life of Santiago, yet retained the absolute confidence of the workers and the poor in his integrity and dedication to their cause.

The Socialist Party shared the Marxist views of the Communist Party, but it was more nationalistic, avoiding the ties to the Soviet Union which the Communist Party maintained through its membership of the Third International. The Socialist Party tended to be further to the left than the Communists in its rejection of capitalism and stress on class warfare, but it cooperated with the Communists and other worker-based parties. Allende was elected to Congress in 1937 and two years later he became Minister of Health in a Popular Front government dominated by the middle-class Radical Party but supported by the Socialist Party and the Communist Party. A major earthquake soon tested his administrative ability, and he gained national recognition for his direction of relief efforts in a disaster which cost 20,000 lives.

The political pendulum continued to swing wildly backward and forward during and after the Second World War. On the one side, the power of the workers continued to grow and forced one concession after another from the ruling classes. Thus, the franchise was gradually expanded and women were finally given the vote. Up to 1949, only 10 percent of the population voted. The proportion was up to 19 percent by 1957 and to 25 percent by 1961. In 1970 the literacy test was abolished and the voting age reduced to 18. On the other side, when the workers sought to translate their voting strength into control of the organs of government, the law of power took precedence over the power of law. In 1948, for example, after municipal elections which revealed overwhelming support for the Communist Party among coal, nitrate and copper miners, the Communist Party was outlawed and its 40,000 to 50,000 members were struck from the register of voters. Thousands were arrested and deported to a small town in the northern desert. Pablo Neruda was ejected from the Senate. In 1957, when students rioted to protest a government decision to raise bus fares, they precipitated a massive demonstration of the dissatisfaction seething in the urban slums. The army was called out to quell the riots and it killed between forty and sixty people in the process. In 1966 workers at El Teniente copper mine struck for higher wages and were joined by the other mines in a sympathy strike which was declared illegal by the government. The army was again brought into action. It killed six mine workers and two women. Similar scenes recurred in 1967 and 1969. A new element had now been added to the ruthlessness earlier instilled by German officers. The armed forces had been taught by Pentagon mentors up-to-date methods of riot control involving helicopters, tear gas, crowd-control tanks and guns. They killed seven civilians, including four children, in Santiago in the 1967 operations, nine at Puerto Montt in 1969.

During the quarter-century following the Second World War major changes took place in the economy of Chile, as in the economies of most countries of Latin America. These changes played a decisive part in the evolution of the class struggle and its intensification. During the war, Britain and the other major European investors were forced to liquidate most of their holdings in Latin America, thereby vastly increasing the economic power of the United States throughout the hemisphere and opening the way to complete its domination. The result was a massive growth in the operations of the transnational companies which are the most characteristic elements of contemporary capitalism.

The transnationals are all based in one or other of the major industrial nations, Britain, West Germany, France, Italy, Japan, but with by far the greatest concentration in the United States. Each of them operates in many countries, distributing their assets and their activities in such a way as to make them independent of the countries in which they are operating. A study of the present situation and the outlook for the transnationals published in 1972 by the Conference Board, a United States-based, business-sponsored, nonprofit research organization stresses these aspects. Of a current gross world product of $3 trillion, one third is produced in the United States, one third in the industrial nations of Europe, Canada, Japan and Australia, and the final third in the rest of the world, which includes the Soviet Union and its satellites and China. Transnationals already account for 15 percent of this world production, that is to say, $450 billion. Of this total, $200 billion is produced by transnationals based in the United States, another $100 billion by foreign-based companies which also operate in the United States, and the balance by interproduction in other countries. The proportion of the world's gross national product contributed by transnationals is growing at a rate of 10 percent annually, and at this rate they will generate one half of all world production in less than 30 years.[5]

The expansion of the transnationals brought to Chile by the 1960s more than a hundred companies or agencies of United States interests, 50 of them being wholly owned subsidiaries. They included most of the big names: Bethlehem Steel in iron, Marcona Corporation and Diamond Crystal Company in salt, Grace, General Mills, Ralston Purina, Coca-Cola and Pepsico in manufactured foodstuffs, Dow, Monsanto and Grace in petrochemicals, Xerox, Sperry Rand, Remington and National Cash Register in office equipment, Grace and Sherwin Williams in paint, Koppers and Johns Manville in cement, Dupont and Atlas

Powder Company in explosives, RCA, ITT, and General Telephone and Electronics in radio and television, Studebaker, Chrysler, Ford and General Motors in automobiles, Firestone and General Tire in rubber tires, General Electric and Grace in electric lamps, Armco Steel, Textron, Kaiser, Koppers, Singer Sewing Machine, Hoover, North American Rockwell and Grace in iron and steel products, General Cables, Phelps Dodge and Northern Indiana Brass in copper fabricating, Standard Oil, Mobil, International Basic Economy Corporation, Phillips Petroleum, Gulf and Texaco in oil distribution, Sterling Drugs, Parke Davis, Schering, Abbott Laboratories, Bristol Myers, Pfizer, Squibb, Wyeth, Upjohn and American Cyanamid in pharmaceuticals, ITT, Grace and Braniff in utilities and transportation, J. Walter Thompson, Grant Advertising, McCann-Erickson and Kenyon and Eckhardt in advertising, Bank of America, First National City, International Basic Economy Corporation, John Hancock Mutual Life, Home Insurance Company and Great American Insurance Company in banking and finance, the eight principal United States producers of movies accounting between them for 65 percent of all playing time in all Chilean theaters, Dun and Bradstreet, Price Waterhouse, Arthur Young and International Basic Economy Corporation in management and accounting services, ITT's Sheraton Hotels and Holiday Inns in tourism, and such others as Gillette, Proctor and Gamble, Chemway, Crown Cork, Air Reduction Company, Kodak, General Dynamics, Ingersoll Rand, Worthington, Continental Can and Manpower.

The significance of this growth of transnationals was stressed by Salvador Allende in an address to the United Nations in New York in December 1972. "The power of these corporations is so great as to transcend all frontiers. The foreign investments of United States companies alone, which today amounts to $32 billion, grew by ten percent annually between 1950 and 1970, while United States exports rose by only five percent. The profits of such companies are fabulous and represent an enormous drain on the resources of the developing countries. In one year, these enterprises repatriated profits from the Third World representing net transfers in their favor of $1.7 billion: $1 billion from Latin America, $280 million from Africa, $366 million from the Far East, and $64 million from the Middle East. Their influence and sphere of action are rudely transforming traditional practices in international trade, transfer of technology, transmission of resources among nations, and labor relations.

"We are witnessing a pitched battle between the great transnational corporations and sovereign states, for the fundamental political, economic and military decisions of these states are being interfered with by worldwide organizations which are not dependent on any state, and which—as regards the sum total of their activities—are not accountable to or regulated by any parliament or institution representing the collective interest. In a word, the entire political structure of the world is being undermined."

This radical domination of the economy of Chile—and of the economies of most countries of Latin America—was carried out under the guise of a theory which insisted that the process would principally benefit the receiving countries and enable them to provide decent living levels for all their people. The theory was elaborated by economists steeped in the traditions of capitalism as practiced in the highly industrialized countries, the beneficiaries of the system. According to their analysis of world problems, the poor countries were poor simply because they had lagged behind in the race to modernize which the industrial countries had already won. But they could save themselves much effort and time by simply imitating the methods already established by the industrial countries. These countries would even help them to start by providing capital and know-how at nominal cost. That was the moral thing to do, and in addition it expressed the enlightened self-interest of the givers. In a world in which everyone was prosperous, there would be more wealth for all to share, and the threat of war would surely diminish as the need for it disappeared.

This approach to development was formalized in the Alliance for Progress. The charter of the Alliance, signed by the United States and all the Latin American republics except Cuba in August 1961 committed the signatories to a total cooperative effort in which all the resources of the hemisphere would be marshalled to ensure as quickly as possible the good life for all the inhabitants. Social objectives were particularly stressed, with a specific affirmation of the urgency of radical land reform.

Whether the United States ever intended to implement the altruistic promises of the Alliance is still in dispute. President John F. Kennedy, who made the commitments, was assassinated in 1963 before any major programs could be implemented. The new administration began immediately a program of distortions and reversals. The social objectives were quickly buried, especially the programs for land reform which had begun to stir deep tensions in most countries the moment they had been announced. The proportion of aid given as gifts was steadily reduced, and the rates of interest on loans were raised close to commercial levels. Aid was tied to procurement of machinery and supplies in the United States, even when more suitable equipment at lower prices was obtainable elsewhere.

The net result was that in Chile, as elsewhere, the promises of the Alliance were quickly frustrated. All it did was to provide further leverage for the transnational companies based in the United States to take over Chilean industry, banking and trade. An agricultural census taken in 1955 revealed that 9.7 percent of the landowners held 86 percent of the country's arable land, and that in three

46

of the most fertile provinces—Santiago, Valparaiso and Aconcagua—a mere 7 percent monopolized 92 percent of the land. At the other end of the spectrum, 74.6 percent of landholders had such tiny plots that they accounted for only 5.3 percent of the land. Ten years later, that situation was unchanged. And as long as it remained unchanged, it was very difficult to influence the political system. The big landowners could maintain their power by controlling the votes of the rural population which depended on them for survival.

Instead of improving, the lot of Chilean workers deteriorated during this period of purported progress. Between 1940 and 1954 there was a regressive redistribution of total income at the expense of the lower-income groups, with wages declining from 27 percent to 21 percent of the national income and the economic gap between rich and poor growing proportionately. This situation, too, continued in the 1960s under the Alliance programs.

During all this period, Salvador Allende as head of the Socialist Party continued to plead the cause of organized labor and other exploited groups. He ran for election to the presidency for the first time in 1952, with the banned Communist Party supporting him from underground, but received only 5.4 percent of the votes cast. At the next presidential elections, six years later, the ban on the Communist Party had been lifted and worker organization had improved greatly. This made Allende a serious contender. The conservative candidate, Jorge Alessandri, won by a narrow margin in a hotly contested election.

By this time, the Christian Democrats headed by Eduardo Frei were coming into prominence. Frei had pioneered in the 1930s in breaking the emotional links that bound the Catholic church in Chile to the oligarchs, and he had continued in the subsequent decades to identify emotionally with the poor masses who were struggling to emancipate themselves from their historic oppression.

47

He understood the institutional barriers which blocked their efforts. He did not accuse the poor of being lazy and ignorant but rather discussed poverty and repression in social terms. Nevertheless, he carried with him from his earlier indoctrination a resistance to socialism which prevented him from mentioning the word even though his rhetoric was socialist. The solution he envisaged for Chile was a welfare state modeled on economic and social structures developed in much of Western Europe after World War II, a state in which all the classes would cooperate so that the workers would share power over national decisions and enjoy a bigger share of the national wealth. For Chile, this was a left-of-center political position, but to the right of the Communist Party and the Socialist Party. Specifically, Frei was committed to the theory of developmentalism. While recognizing that it had not progressed very far since it had been proposed in the late 1940s, he insisted that a government truly dedicated to the interests of the people—not to those of the upper class—could make it work by channeling the energies and resources of the country into types of economic production that would benefit both rich and poor. To do this, he argued, it was necessary only to end the private control (though not necessarily the private ownership) of the means of production, so that the state could plan freely, determine goals and allocate priorities.

The holders of power in Chile had no desire to change anything, but the extraordinary strength revealed by Allende in the 1958 elections caused many of them to look to the Christian Democrats as a necessary evil. It was clear to them that the Left would soon have an absolute and irreversible majority in a straight contest with the Right. Not more than five percent of Chileans belonged to the wealthy groups of landowners, merchants, bankers and professionals, and at most a further 30 percent were middle-class: tradesmen, store owners, civil servants, small businessmen and white-collar employees. Even the state employees—and 12 percent of all Chileans work for the government—had no overwhelming commitment to or interest in private enterprise. The bogey of communism, long fostered by the media of communications and the church, was losing its impact, and once that went, there was no reason why they would not accept a socialist government. The only hope of shifting the balance was to present a moderate Leftist, like Eduardo Frei, who could siphon off a substantial part of the vote that would otherwise go to Allende.

The Christian Democrats had close links to the Catholic church in every country in which the party had been established, and important sectors of the Chilean church joined in the plans to "stop communism" by giving the presidency to Frei in 1964. David E. Mutchler, who as a Jesuit student engaged in historical research in Chile had access to many of the people involved in the strategy and to many of their internal memoranda and other documents, says that the Chilean bishops had seen as early as 1956 the threat of an Allende victory some time in the future. In that year they petitioned the Jesuit General in Rome to send social scientists to Chile. One of those he sent was a Belgian Jesuit named Roger Vekemans who soon became a key figure in the campaign to stop Allende. Vekemans developed a series of programs designed to win votes for Frei, some of them funded by a West German aid agency, others by United States groups who later were revealed to have been funded by the CIA.[6] It also emerged later that ITT and various agencies of the United States government—including the CIA—poured large sums of money into the Frei campaign. Frei won easily in 1964, with 56.1 percent of the vote against 38.9 percent for the left coalition headed by Allende.

Frei's record in office fell far short of his promise. He was able to put through Congress, in spite of conservative opposition, a far-reaching land reform law. It authorized the state to expropriate not only abandoned or under-utilized land, as the previous law had done, but all land belonging to a single owner in excess of 200 acres of irrigated land or its equivalent. Most of the payment was to be in bonds payable over a number of years, the land value to be determined by the land reform agency, with appeal procedures if the owner was not satisfied. The law provided that the peasants who lived and worked on an expropriated farm would continue to do so during a three-year period of training in proper methods of production. At the end of the period, the peasants would each get his own holding and would pay for it over 30 years. The government promised to give land to 100,000 of the 350,000 peasant families in the country by 1970, a goal which officials of the UN's Food and Agriculture Organization regarded as ambitious but feasible. In fact, at the end of five years of the Frei mandate, only 15,000 families had benefited, and the process had ground to a halt as the government struggled to reconcile the conflicting demands of peasants frustrated by delays and landowners organized to retain possession of all their productive land.

The principal reason for this poor showing, one that takes us to the very center of the problems of Chile, was that Frei was afraid to challenge the landowners even though he had the legal weapons to do so. Accordingly, he left them their best lands and took over mostly land that was unirrigated and lacking in capital infrastructure, requiring substantial investment to make it productive. He consequently ran out of funds.

Frei's other major commitment was the "Chileaniza-tion" of the big copper companies, but this also turned out to be less of a victory than it at first appeared. In 1967, Chile bought a 51 percent interest in the El Teniente mine owned by Kennecott, paying $80 million over two years. Kennecott agreed to lend this money to the State Copper

Corporation to help finance an expansion program that would raise output from 180,000 to 280,000 tons by 1970. Chile would lend an additional $20 million to the new company and would guarantee repayment of a further $100 million to be obtained from international lending agencies. In this way, Kennecott would be able to almost double its capacity without putting up any new capital. To sweeten the deal still further, the effective tax rate on Kennecott was cut from 86 to 44 percent, and it was to continue to control all mining and processing operations, as well as sales, by means of a management contract.

Anaconda made no equity sale in 1965 in its two major subsidiaries but agreed to split ownership of all future ventures in Chile, and to expand its output by 53 percent between 1965 and 1970. It sold Chile a 25 percent interest in a third mine then being developed and scheduled to come into substantial production in the 1970s, La Exotica. As part of the deal, Anaconda's tax rates were reduced from 70 percent to an average—on the three mines—of 53 percent. The third big United States company, the Cerro Corporation, sold a 25 percent—and later a 30 percent —interest in its new mine, Rio Blanco. Its tax rate was reduced to 53 percent.

While the Frei government hailed the conclusion of these various agreements as an enormous step toward freeing the country from the domination of a copper industry over which it exercised no control, Chilean and other economists were quick to point out that the benefits were more apparent than real. Kennecott gave an indication of its own evaluation in its 1967 annual report to its shareholders, assuring them that this new "partnership arrangement" had been entered into "voluntarily and enthusiastically," and that it would be "mutually advantageous."

What that means was made clearer in an analysis made by the United States Department of Commerce, which concluded that, while increasing gross receipts from increased production, Chile suffered a 16 percent reduction in earnings per ton of copper produced.[7] Another analyst reported that a calculation of the benefits and the costs of each transaction for the companies and for the Chilean government established that only in the case of Cerro were the net benefits to Chile greater than those won by the copper producing companies.[8]

One reason for this result was that Chile paid too much for its share of the assets. Kennecott's El Teniente mine, for example, was listed in Kennecott's books as worth $65.7 million, but Chile agreed to pay $81.6 million for its 51 percent share. In addition, Chile gave major benefits to the companies in the form of tax exemptions and low-interest loans. The government's total revenue participation, now partly in taxes and partly in dividends on its equity in the companies, as a share of "returned value" dropped from 64 percent in 1964 to 57 percent in 1969.[9] Yet another issue resolved in favor of the copper companies was their right to fix the so-called New York price on which the copper was valued for export and for all tax and profit calculations. This price had fluctuated over the years in sympathy with the world price as established by the London Metal Exchange, but almost invariably with a wide margin between the two prices. Moreover, Chile had no effective voice in determining it. In 1952, for example, the New York price was 25 cents a pound; the London price, 32 cents; in 1966, 54 and 69 cents; in 1970, 56 and 72 cents.

Frei's "Chileanization" was by no means the first attempt by Chile to establish a relationship with the copper companies which would ensure to Chile a fair share of the profits of the enterprise. When the Korean War raised demand for copper, the United States imposed a price ceiling of 24.5 cents a pound, to which the government of Chile reacted in 1952 with legislation authorizing the Central Bank to sell all Chilean copper abroad, giving the

President power to increase the proportion of copper to be refined in Chile, and adjusting taxes on copper in Chile's favor. The short-term benefits were significant. Chile could for the first time sell copper in Western Europe, 6,000 tons in 1953, nearly 200,000 in 1955. The companies reacted rapidly and ruthlessly. Production in Chile fell 8 percent between 1949 and 1954, while world production and demand were expanding rapidly, so that Chile's share in world production dropped from 21 percent in 1948 to 11.6 percent in 1953-54. Needed capital outlays in Chile were postponed, resulting in net disinvestment, while new capital was pumped into marginal mines in Montana and Utah. Finally, local expenditures in the form of wages were cut by a program of importing capital-intensive factors of production, such as bigger electrical shovels, resulting in a decline of employment in the sector of big mines (the *Gran Minería*) from 17,385 in 1945 to 11,057 in 1954. All of this occurred in spite of the fact that Chile's production costs were significantly below those of the alternative sources to which the American companies turned in their determination to reassert their control of the decision-making processes.

In 1955, the Chilean government submitted. A new law gave the companies lower taxes, accelerated depreciation and provided more favorable exchange rates, in return for a promise of higher revenues through increased production. The companies responded by capital outlays of $200 million (almost all provided from retained earnings), which brought some increase in production, but at the cost of a drastic fall in government copper revenues. In 1955, taxation of the copper firms brought in $156 million; in 1961, only $68 million.

The failure of Frei's agreements with the copper companies to give Chile any significant improvement had become so apparent by 1968 that Congress enacted a law providing that all income obtained in large-scale mining from the rise in copper prices above 29 cents per pound should go to Chile. Frei, however, ruled that Congress was not entitled to change the contracts he had negotiated and refused to implement its instructions.[10]

In 1969, Frei caused some surprise and brought himself some political benefit by an agreement with Anaconda to purchase 51 percent of its two biggest mines, Chuquicamata and El Salvador, with an option to buy the remaining 49 percent under certain conditions between 1972 and 1980. Anaconda, far more dependent on Chile for its total copper supplies than Kennecott and Cerro, had fought Chileanization successfully in 1964. By 1969, it had apparently been convinced by rising feeling within Chile that its survival depended on lowering its profile, perhaps also impressed by the benefits gained by its competitors from their partnerships, and satisfied that its management contract under the new arrangement would enable it to cintinue to call the shots. From the point of view of the average Chilean, this contract was no more beneficial than the earlier ones. He remained convinced that nothing would change in Chile until the domination of the economy by the foreign copper companies was ended.

It was ultimately this recognition of economic dependence resulting from a capitalistic system which denied them a fair share of the benefits of their own economy that persuaded an overwhelming majority of politically conscious Chileans to vote for a president who promised to start the country on the road to socialism.

As they looked back over the seventy years of the twentieth century, they could see an enormous increase in the amount of wealth generated in their country, but no corresponding benefit to themselves. No matter how they had tried, they had found themselves each year more dependent on decisions over which they had lacked control. In one sense, they had been fortunate. When the demand for their nitrates had declined disastrously as a result of the advances made in creating artificial substitutes by the Germans during two world wars, this decline had been soon compensated by bigger demand for copper. But in spite of all their efforts and entreaties, the copper magnates—like the nitrate magnates before them—had made no effort to utilize the profits to create a balanced and self-supporting economy. Instead, as a miner had put it, they took the copper and left a hole in the ground. As the population grew, it was possible to increase the imports of food instead of reforming the agricultural system and using the land available in abundance but underutilized. The increase in income from mining from 1945 to 1970 was paralleled by the increase in the quantity of food imported.

It is easy for the outside observer to moralize about the stupidity and shortsightedness of Chilean rulers. He must, however, recognize that those who monopolized power were willing cooperators in a system which worked well for them. The modern sector of Chile was extremely progressive by Latin American measures, with high levels of education, good health facilities, all the trappings of enlightened democracy. In addition, while the appearances of power remained with the oligarchs, the reality had in fact passed during the quarter-century following World War II from this group to the transnationals. The Yarur Family, the giant of the textile industry, had become an associate of W. R. Grace. The Edwards Family was involved with Rockefeller's International Basic Economy Corporation, with Ralston Purina, and with other United States interests. A study of the affiliations of 285 Chilean officers and directors of the 50 largest nonfinancial corporations during the mid-1960s revealed that four interest groups of Chilean families controlled 21 of the top 50 corporations, and that two-thirds of the officers and 21 of the top 50 had either personal or close family ties to foreign interests.[11]

Other important sectors of society were also drawn into the foreign orbit. Transnationals bring in many of their own management people and scientists when they first penetrate a country, but political and economic reasons encourage them to build up quickly an intermediate layer of national administrators and technicians, and to cultivate government officials and politicians. It was long the practice in Chile for certain categories of Chilean employees of foreign firms to be paid in dollars which they could transfer abroad or convert in the black market into local currency, a practice ended only during the Allende presidency. This group tended to identify in all respects with United States interests and form the base of opposition to social change. Penetration of the political world was possible by directorates, consulting fees and professional engagements. Washington columnist Jack Anderson identified Arturo Matte as a co-conspirator with ITT and the CIA in the efforts to prevent Allende from taking office in 1970. Matte's family is associated with that of former President Jorge Alessandri who ran second in the 1970 elections and consequently was next in line for the presidency if Allende could be eliminated. Dragomir Tomic, brother of the Christian Democrat candidate for president in 1970 (Radomiro Tomic), was a member of Anaconda's team of lawyers for its Chuquicamata properties. Rodolfo Mitchells became a vice-president of Anaconda after he had been a senator for the Radical Party.[12]

The speeding up of all the processes of society which characterizes our present technological and cybernetic era accelerated enormously the changes occurring in Chile during the 1950s and 1960s. The system worked inexorably to concentrate the benefits of production in the hands of those who already had more than their share. The average worker in 1956 was able with one hour of labor to buy a kilo of green vegetables, or a kilo of sugar, or a liter of milk. In 1965, he had to work a little more than two hours to obtain the same benefit, and four years later he had to work for more than three hours. The average worker, married and with one child eight years old, spent 66.8 percent of his earnings on food in 1965, but in 1969 he would have to spend 82.3 percent in order to maintain the diet established as standard minimum by United Nations experts. In practice, because of the other demands on his income, he did not reach the dietary minimum. "Instead, bread and a mixture of flour and water were substituted for more nutritious fare. The result was massive malnutrition, which in working-class areas was often so severe as to cause brain damage."[13]

The disastrous condition of the worker was only part of the failure of the Christian Democrats to remedy the social ills of Chile without attacking the structural problems which had caused them. Simultaneously, thanks to the growth of population at a more rapid rate than the opportunities for work, the army of unemployed and subemployed was also growing. The total result was a relentless pressure for more extreme measures to change the quality of life by changing the basic rules of the game, a pressure which expressed itself in the plurality for the coalition headed by Salvador Allende in the 1970 presidential elections.

2.

Chile Opts for Socialism

Even with hindsight, it is still not clear why the oligarchy failed to create a coalition in 1970 which would unite the opposition to Allende, as they had done successfully in 1964. No doubt the evolution of the Christian Democrats while in power was a significant factor. The program on which they took office was a very progressive one. Many of them were skilled economists. They understood that Chile had complicated structural problems, that maldistribution of land and income resulted inevitably in low levels of purchasing power and of agricultural production. They knew that the rich would stop sending their wealth abroad or investing it in industries producing luxury items for a limited market only when socially more desirable ways for using this wealth were also made economically more attractive to the business community.

They started out very well with their ambitious program of land reform. And their commitment to the principle of freedom did in fact produce a revolutionary change in the Chilean countryside. A labor law voted in 1967 eliminated many restrictions on peasant unions and brought about a remarkable growth in the number of unionized rural workers almost immediately, an increase of 60 percent to 83,000 in twelve months. These workers simultaneously acquired a consciousness of their own power and developed their own internal leadership, becoming for the first time a political power in the country. But Frei had come to power with the backing of the Right, and he was unwilling to encourage changes that would lose him that support. His party was a minority in Congress and needed the rightist coalition to govern. In consequence, the land reform program ground to a halt. Tax reform and banking reform did not get beyond the talking stage. The Chileanization of copper left Chile with less revenue from that source than before. Such increase as occurred in economic activity resulted from renegotiation of old foreign debts and assumption of new foreign obligations, postponing to the next administration the problems of repayment. This millstone of debt was to prove Allende's undoing, for it was the weapon used by his domestic and foreign enemies to produce economic chaos and provide the pretext for the military intervention.

The steady withdrawal of President Frei from the progressive program of the Christian Democrats inevitably produced conflict within the party, leading in May 1969 to the resignation of some of its most dynamic members. "The most advanced current of Christian thought is no longer picked up by us," said Senator Agustín Gumucio, explaining his resignation. "Instead, rather than an instrument of revolutionary change, we are an instrument of the status quo, an administrator of the system, guarantor of the established order."[1] The dissidents formed a community action movement which soon became a political party, the Popular Action Movement (MAPU). It never acquired a very big following, but it was influential in making Catholics conscious of the conflict between their principles and Chilean capitalism, and in helping to start a search among Christians at the philosophical and theological level into the bases for their traditional opposition to socialism and into the possibility of cooperation between Christians and Marxists.

Even in Chile, a country strongly Roman Catholic and with a higher level of religious practice than most Latin American countries, such issues could be debated with total freedom after the revolutionary documents promulgated by the bishops of Latin America at Medellin, Colombia, in 1968. These documents are particularly illuminating because they reveal the search for new approaches to the social and economic order agitating the Catholic church throughout the hemisphere. The analysis they present of the social, economic and political situation of Latin America is clearly Marxist, but the solution proposed by the bishops returns to the previous official position of the church, a position which was also the official stand of the Christian Democrats in Chile and elsewhere. The analysis reflects the impact on the bishops of progressive theologians who had built up a continental network for exchange of their ideas while in Rome for the Second Vatican Council between 1962 and 1965. These theologians stressed the importance for the church's survival of a withdrawal from its traditional dependence on the wealthy and a commitment to creating human living conditions for the marginal masses. The bishops borrowed from the "theology of liberation" they had developed the marxist language and concepts by means of which it explained the social ills of Latin America.

When they turned to solutions, nevertheless, the bishops at Medellin rejected equally "the liberal capitalist system" and "the temptation of the Marxist system." Instead, they called for a restructuring of the economy according to "the directives of the social magisterium of the church." What this somewhat vague expression meant for them was spelled out in a passage that showed they had in mind the corporate state as projected in papal encyclicals from Leo XIII to Pius XI. "We make an urgent appeal to business-men and their organizations, as well as to the political authorities, to modify radically their system of values, their attitudes and methods as they affect the purpose, organization and operation of their enterprises. Those en-trepreneurs who individually or through their organiza-tions try to operate their business in accordance with the directives of the social doctrine of the church deserve every support. Only through such initiatives can social and economic change in Latin America be directed toward a truly human economy."

The MAPU leaders, who included leading Catholic priests and theologians, hailed the Medellín analysis as expressing exactly the situation in Chile, while insisting that the proposed solution had been tried and had not worked. They argued that a growing number of Catholic thinkers around the world, people like Jordan Bishop in neighboring Bolivia and José María González Ruiz in Spain, had reached the conclusion that the Marxist analy-sis—in particular, its insistence on class warfare as a fact—alone provided the key to understanding the social, eco-nomic and political reality of dependent countries like Chile, and that far from denying the Christian approach, that of Marxism complements it. The impact of these Catholics on thinking Chileans was reinforced by the paral-lel efforts of the progressive Protestant ISAL, which in a new spirit of ecumenism worked closely with progressive Catholics. All of this had a definite impact on the voting in 1970, neutralizing to some extent the right-wing propa-ganda which sought to enlist Catholics in a crusade against "godless communism."[2]

The main weight of the Catholic church continued, nevertheless, to lean toward the Christian Democrats or the conservative National Party. And the other forces that had opposed Allende successfully in 1958 and 1964 also continued in place. These included big business, both national and foreign, and the many agencies of the United States which were in a position to influence Chilean opinion. It is now a matter of clear record that Frei's election campaign in 1964 was underwritten in large part by the United States in government loans, Alliance for Progress expenditures, and private company funds. In a report to the Subcommittee on Foreign Aid, Senator Ernest Gruening of Alaska wrote: "Clearly the 1964 financial assistance package must have been based solely on political considerations—to maintain Chile's current levels of economic activity and investment and to support the balance of payments so that financial deterioration and unemployment would not occur in an election year." *Engineering and Mining Journal*, a publication which can be assumed to know what the mining giants are doing, noted in November 1964 that "privately, top Washington officials admit Frei's election was greatly helped by the 'serious efforts' of United States copper interests aiding the U.S. Information Agency."[3] David E. Mutchler has put on the record original documents revealing programs designed to help Frei funded by such disparate sponsors as church-related foundations in Europe and the CIA.[4]

All these right-wing forces apparently reached the conclusion, incorrectly as the event proved, that they could win the presidency in 1970 without help from the Christian Democrats. In 1969, the National Security Council of the United States developed in Memo #19, the text of which was never made public, a strategy for overthrowing Salvador Allende if he should come to power. But the Council, representing the combined thinking of the CIA, the Pentagon and the State Department, approached the problem on the assumption that Allende could only come to power by using violence, apparently having concluded that the electoral approach would continue to fail him.

Part of the reason for the confidence of the Right was the ideological division within the Left parties and groups. The two main members of the six-party coalition which carried Allende to power in 1970, the Socialist and Communist parties, had always maintained distinct ideological lines. The Communist Party generally followed the Soviet line, while the Socialist Party tended to be more militantly aggressive. They came together tactically from 1938 to 1941 in the Popular Front, a coalition in which they were junior partners. The Communist Party was outlawed from 1948 to 1958, and it worked underground in favor of Allende's candidacy as a Socialist in 1958. When the ban was removed, it joined openly with the Socialist Party in the UP coalition which pitted Allende against Frei in 1964. Ideological and tactical divisions, nevertheless, persisted between the two parties, and there was considerable public disagreement before the coalition came together on a presidential candidate for 1970.

Another reason that may have reduced the concern of the opposing groups was the adhesion of the nonmarxist Radical Party to the UP coalition. This group of middle-class Chileans and small businessmen had supported Alessandri in 1958 and Frei in 1964. Its interests were middle-of-the-road and middle-of-the-spectrum. It would act as a brake on Allende's extremism, would surely desert him if he refused to be reasonable. Even after Allende won a plurality in the three-way race, this still seemed to be the attitude of the U.S. State Department. When urged by ITT to act to prevent Allende's inauguration, it opted for a low profile, presumably satisfied that the objective would be more easily secured by letting him turn for a time slowly in the wind.

ITT had a greater sense of urgency than the State Department. It had substantial assets in jeopardy, including the telephone company which provided most of the country's service and which it claimed was worth $153 million. As Washington columnist Jack N. Anderson revealed in March 1972, causing a sensation around the world, it exerted immediate and massive pressures on the State Department, the CIA, the United States Ambassador in Chile, and Chilean rightists. The correspondence in the United States took place at the highest level, Harold Geneen, president of ITT, and his top aides speaking for the company, and having access to presidential adviser Henry Kissinger (now Secretary of State), Secretary of State William Rogers, and the head of the CIA. This last contact was facilitated by John A. McCone, former head of the CIA and in 1970 simultaneously a vice-president of ITT and a consultant to the CIA.

The first letters, written between September 14 and 21, 1970, reflect optimism that Allende could be denied the fruits of his victory. In Chile, if no presidential candidate wins an absolute majority, the two houses of Congress in a joint session choose either the leader or the runner-up. Although the unbroken tradition had always given the presidency to the leader, the ITT strategists believed they could persuade the Christian Democrats to throw their votes to the runner-up. This involved an elaborate horse trade known as the Alessandri Formula, under which Alessandri would resign if elected, paving the way for new elections. Frei would be eligible to run in these elections, and ITT was confident he would win over Allende in a straight contest. Alessandri in fact made a public announcement that he would resign if elected.

The Anderson revelations further established that ITT had offered the State Department financial assistance "in sums up to seven figures" to enable it to intervene in Chile's internal affairs without having to account for the funds to Congress. Two of Geneen's aides also informed him that within a few days of the first ITT approach to Kissinger's office, "Ambassador Edward Korry finally received a message from the State Department giving him the green light to move in the name of President Nixon, . . . the maximum possible authority to do all possible—short of Dominican Republic-type action—to keep Allende from taking power." The reference to the Dominican Republic meant that American marines were not to be promised.

Simultaneously ITT was moving directly in Chile. It started, along with other United States firms, to "pump some advertising into *El Mercurio*," Santiago's biggest daily owned by the Edwards interests. Augustin Edwards, head of Chile's most powerful economic empire, had long been an implacable foe of Allende. Shortly after the election, he moved to Miami, Florida, and became an international vice-president of the Pepsi Cola Corporation, whose president Donald Kendall is a close friend of President Nixon. Other pressures proposed by ITT included getting back on radio and television some twenty propagandists whom the Edwards and Matte groups had been supporting, having the U.S. Information Service distribute the editorials of *El Mercurio* around Latin America and Europe, and persuading the European press—"through our contacts there"—to give publicity to "the story of what disaster could fall on Chile if Allende and Co. win this country."

As the date for the Congress decision approached and it seemed less certain that Allende would be eliminated, the ITT documents began to evaluate a proposal which they attributed to the State Department for creating economic and political chaos in Chile if the UP government came to power. These proposals are particularly significant because they parallel closely the scenario as it actually developed later. The suggested steps were that banks should not renew credits, that companies should drag their feet in sending money, making deliveries, shipping spare parts, that savings and loan companies already in trouble should be pressured into closing their doors, that companies in a position to do so should suspend operations, and that all United States technical help be withdrawn.

65

As the threat of an Allende assumption of power grew, so did the hysteria. "Chances of thwarting Allende's assumption of power now are pegged mainly to an economic collapse which is being encouraged by some sectors in the business and political community and by President Frei himself. The next two weeks will be decisive in this respect. Cash is in short supply. But the government is printing more money. There is an active black market. . . . Undercover efforts are being made to bring about the bankruptcy of one or two of the major savings and loan associations. This is expected to trigger a run on banks and the closure of some factories, resulting in more unemployment. The pressures resulting from economic chaos could force a major segment of the Christian Democratic party to reconsider their stand in relation to Allende in the Congressional run-off vote. It would become apparent, for instance, that there is no confidence among the business community in Allende's future policies and that the overall health of the nation is at stake. More important, massive unemployment and unrest might produce enough violence to force the military to move."[5]

Further efforts to provoke the military to intervene were also reported. On September 27, an extreme rightist faction launched a series of terrorist acts, mostly bombings, to provoke a backlash from the Left that would bring out the army. On October 9, ITT vice-president William Merriam wrote John McCone: "Approaches continue to be made to select members of the armed forces in an attempt to have them lead some sort of uprising—no success to date." On October 16, ITT's PR director for Latin America, Hal Hendrix wrote to ITT's first vice-president Edward Gerrity: "The chance of a military coup is slim but it continues to exist. . . . A key figure in this possibility is former Brigadier General Roberto Viaux, who last October led an insurrection. . . . Word was passed to Viaux from Washington to hold back last week. It was felt that he was not adequately prepared, his timing was off, and he should 'cool it' for a later, unspecified date. . . . As part of the persuasion to delay, Viaux was given oral assurance he would receive materials, assistance and support from the United States and others for a later maneuver."

When Allende's confirmation had become certain as a result of Alessandri's withdrawal, ITT sent a long letter to Kissinger suggesting ways to neutralize the UP victory. Again, the approach it suggested was the one actually implemented: "All United States aid funds already committed to Chile should be placed in the 'under review' status in order that entry of money into Chile is temporarily stopped with a view to permanent cut-off if necessary."

Testimony subsequently given before a United States Senate subcommittee investigating the activities of multinational corporations confirmed the accuracy of the Anderson revelations and brought out additional facts. The intrigues to stop Allende had begun even before his election. On July 16, 1970, Geneen met with the chief of Clandestine Operations for the Western Hemisphere Division of the CIA, William V. Broe, after which Merriam talked to him "many times" and had "several" luncheons with him. Broe, Merriam testified, agreed to the ITT recommendations which included steps to make Frei again president, to foment violence that would provoke a coup, and to distribute anti-Allende propaganda in other Latin American countries through United States government agencies. Merriam also visited the State Department 25 times and talked frequently with Kissinger and his aides for "a year." He urged the United States government to bring pressure on the World Bank and the Inter-American Development Bank to stop making loans to Chile. He was part of a group formed by Anaconda, and in which Kennecot, Grace, Pfizer, Ralston-Purina and the Bank of America participated, which sought to establish a common policy for dealing with Allende. He made repeated calls to General Motors and to Ford, as well as to banks in New York and California, urging them to stop or reduce their activities in Chile and thus promote "an economic collapse."

One ITT spokesman at the Senate enquiry sought to whitewash the company's activities by claiming that the million dollars offered to the CIA was intended for "constructive" purposes, such as low-cost housing. After hearing conflicting evidence from other witnesses, Senator Frank Church, chairman of the subcommittee, said that it was "obvious that someone is lying, and we must take a very serious view of perjury under oath." He said the transcript would be turned over to the Justice Department for a possible indictment for perjury.[6] In its own report, the subcommittee said: "What is not to be condoned is that the highest officials of the ITT sought to engage the CIA in a plan covertly to manipulate the outcome of the Chilean presidential election. In so doing, the company overstepped the line of acceptable corporate behavior."

The subcommittee report also revealed that, contrary to what many had previously assumed, the Nixon administration had been profoundly involved in the whole process in Chile even before ITT had asked its help. The "Forty Committee," the National Security Council's organ in charge of studying and approving plans for covert action abroad by the CIA and other United States intelligence agencies, had met in June 1970 to discuss Chile. Henry Kissinger presides over this committee which includes the chairman of the joint chiefs of staff, the deputy secretary of Defense, the deputy secretary of State, the director of Central Intelligence, and (until 1972) the attorney general. After the June meeting, CIA director Richard Helms promised McCone an expenditure of $400,000 in CIA funds to assist anti-Allende news media. Helms at that time was pessimistic about Alessandri's chances and believed Allende would win. This was contrary to the official reports coming from the United States Embassy in Santiago, reports which were based on polls commissioned or undertaken by the CIA.

The subcommittee also established that the initiative for a meeting between Broe and Gerrity at the end of September came from the government, and that Broe at that meeting proposed "a plan to accelerate economic chaos in Chile" in order to pressure the Christian Democrats to vote against Allende's ratification as president or weaken his position if chosen. Charles A. Meyer, then assistant secretary of State for inter-American affairs, told the subcommittee that the Forty Committee had met earlier in September for the express purpose of discussing United States policy in connection with Chile, while refusing to reveal what was said at the meeting, what decisions were taken, or what instructions were given to the ambassador in Santiago.

Although these details did not come to light until later, there were already indications at the time of what might be expected. At his first press conference, Allende said he attributed "no significance" to the failure of President Nixon to join Pope Paul and Premier Chou En-lai in sending him a congratulatory message. He also acknowledged the existence of right-wing extremists prepared to violate Chile's traditions of acceptance of the decision made at the polls. His personal security force had already uncovered two plots to kill him, he said. And the arrest of retired General Roberto Viaux Marambio and other suspects in the killing of General René Schneider, Commander-in-Chief, had produced proof of a conspiracy by "the ultra-right and some of the right that is not so ultra."

Allende made it clear, nevertheless, that he was not going to be shaken from his commitments to pursue his policies strictly within constitutional limitations, including the additional restrictions to which he had agreed as part of the price of support by the Christian Democrats in the congressional vote to confirm him as president. "If vio-

69

lence is to come," he said shortly after he was elected, "it will be because the powerful were always the ones who unleashed the violence, shed the blood of Chileans, and blocked the progress of the country."[7]

The program agreed to by all the parties forming UP specified that the Allende government would not create a socialist state but would lay the foundations on which such a state could subsequently be built. The UP victory, it said, "will open the way to the most democratic political regime in the country's history," creating a new power structure "through a process of democratization at all levels and an organized mobilization of the masses."

A first step toward the building of socialism would be to end "the power of national and foreign monopolistic capitalism and of the big landowners." This would involve the establishment of "an area of social property, . . . a dominant state area formed by the enterprises that the state presently possesses along with the enterprises that will be expropriated. The first step will be to nationalize those basic sources of wealth, such as the large mining companies of copper, iron, nitrate and others, which are controlled by foreign capital and internal monopolies. Into this area of nationalized activities will be integrated the following sectors:

1) the large mining companies of copper, nitrate, iodine, iron and coal;
2) the country's financial system, especially private banks and insurance companies;
3) foreign trade;
4) the great distribution enterprises and monopolies;
5) the strategic industrial monopolies;
6) in general, all those activities which determine the country's economic and social development, such as the production and distribution of electrical energy; rail, air and sea transportation; communications; the production, refining and distribution of

petroleum and its derivatives—including bottled gas; iron and steel production; cement; petrochemicals and heavy chemicals, cellulose and paper."[8]

In addition to the area of social property, the program specified areas of private property and of mixed property. The enterprises in the area of private property would be in the majority, consisting of all sectors of industry, mining, agriculture and services other than those which had "controlled the market monopolistically, monopolizing state aid and bank credit and exploiting the other industrial enterprises of the country." Mixed enterprises would have the state as a partner with private enterprise. This arrangement was envisaged for situations in which a manufacturing process involved heavy capitalization and advanced technology.

"We need a new model of the state, of the economy, and of society centered on man, on his needs and aspirations," Allende told the Chileans. The task was extraordinarily complex, he said. "There are no precedents from which to draw inspiration. We set foot on a new road; we march without a guide through unknown terrain, having for a compass only our fidelity to the humanism of the ages—especially Marxist humanism—and having as our guiding star the design of the society we desire, inspired by the deepest longings of the people of Chile."[9]

Allende understood very well the enormity of the task he had undertaken, as well as the need for it, and he wanted everyone to be clear about this. "The real reasons for our backwardness are to be found in the system," he said in his first major address after taking office, "in this capitalist-dependent system which counterposes the rich minority to the needy majority internally and the powerful nations to the poor nations externally, a system in which the many make possible the prosperity of the few.

"We have received a society torn by social inequality; a society divided into antagonistic classes of the exploited

71

and exploiting; a society in which violence is a part of the institutions themselves which condemn man to a never-satisfied greed, the most inhuman form of cruelty and indifference in the face of the suffering of others. We have inherited a society wracked by unemployment, which throws growing numbers of the citizenry into a situation of forced idleness and poverty. These masses are not, as some say, the result of overpopulation; rather, with their tragic destiny, they are living witnesses to the inability of the regime to guarantee everyone the elementary right to work.

"We have received an economy plagued by inflation—which, month after month, eats up the miserable wages of the workers, leaving them with next to nothing to live on in the last years of their lives, when they reach the end of an existence of privation. The working people of Chile are bleeding through this wound, and it will be difficult to heal. But we are confident we will be able to heal it, because the economic policy of the government will, from now on, be aimed at serving the interests of the people.

"We have received a dependent society, one whose basic sources of income were alienated by the internal allies of the great international firms. We are dependent in the economic, cultural, technological and political fields. We have inherited a society which has seen its most deeply felt desire of independent development frustrated, a divided society in which the majority of families are denied the right to work, education, health care, recreation and even the hope of a better future."[10]

The Chilean constitution gives the president far more discretionary power than does that of the United States, placing the presidency on a higher level than Congress. The conditions imposed by the Christian Democrats on Allende in return for their support of his candidacy were designed to correct that imbalance and make it impossible for Allende as president to take any action not approved by

Congress. Perhaps the most important of the conditions concerned the armed forces, removing them in effect from the president's control. It was agreed that "the organic structures and hierarchies of the Armed Forces and Carabineros [national police] be respected, the systems of selection, prerequisites, and disciplinary norms now existing; that these groups be assured of adequate equipment for their mission as watchmen of the national security, and that their work on national development not be used to reroute their specific functions, nor compromise their budgets, nor create armed organizations parallel to the Armed Forces and Carabineros."[11]

Other new safeguards established were designed to strengthen university autonomy, protect freedom of speech and prevent the government from dominating the information media. Although unexceptionable in principle, the new laws in practice tended to protect the status quo and to perpetuate the traditional preponderance of newspapers and magazines owned by and expressing the views of big business. The one significant change was in relation to television. There had previously been acceptance of a state monopoly, but now it seemed desirable to create an alternative, since for the first time the state system would be controlled by a left-wing regime. Accordingly, the University of Chile and the Catholic University were authorized to join in establishing a network to cover the entire country. A television council was established for "general orientation, vigilance and control" of the medium, its head to be named by the President with the approval of Congress. Further, "all intervention by government through television in order to express ideas, proposals, or successes, will give the right to reply to political parties of the opposition with equal scheduling and time. The time given to reply will be divided by the opposition parties in proportion to the parliamentary representatives that they have."[12]

73

Allende's need to work within the constitution and his pre-electoral commitments were not his only problem. Pushing him from the other side was the Movement of the Revolutionary Left (MIR), a small but highly disciplined, militant and dynamic organization with its principal base in the shantytowns surrounding Santiago and among the peasants and Mapuche Indians of the south. In an evaluation of the UP victory published in October 1970, it expressed its belief that the UP program hit at "some vital nuclei of capitalism, such as foreign enterprises, finance capital, industrial monopolies and big estates. We also believe that if this program is implemented it will create a bourgeois and imperialist counteroffensive which, given the energies and aspirations of the working class, will bring about a quick radicalization of the process. For these reasons, although the UP program is not identical to ours, we shall push and support the realization of those measures."

MIR was willing to support Allende, but not because it believed he could win. Their difference on that issue is one that has long agitated Marxism and is going to be more acutely debated than ever before as a result of the failure of the Allende experiment. Both sides knew that Marx had not excluded the possibility of a peaceful transition to socialism, even if no example of the process had yet been recorded. But they differed on the circumstances in which this could take place. "We have never discarded the possibility," said the MIR statement, "that a country may pass to socialism as a 'ripe fruit' when the worldwide capitalist system is in agony and socialism prevails on this planet. This is not the present situation."

In consequence, the primary purpose of MIR's support was to provoke the "imperialist counteroffensive" and thus "radicalize" the process. "We have always affirmed that the seizing of power by the workers will be possible only through armed struggle. We know that powerful interests must be hurt, interests which in each country are protected by the capitalist state apparatus; we also know that the ruling classes, as taught by historical experience, will not hesitate to use violence in defense of their power and wealth." The armed struggle, MIR further believed, would not be a quick insurrection that would turn power over definitely to the workers, but "a long and irregular revolutionary war" for which the workers should prepare by arming themselves, demonstrating, rioting, fighting in the streets, encouraging the seizure of land by peasants, of factories by workers, of houses by the homeless. For these reasons, MIR said, it would maintain its "political and military structure as long as the capitalist system prevails in Chile and as long as power is not effectively controlled by the workers."

The logic of MIR's analysis forced it at all times to press Allende to move faster than he was moving at any given moment. It also encouraged situations of challenge when he sought diplomatic give-and-take. To the threatened oligarchs, the MIR was always the tail wagging the dog, the totalitarian revolution just one step away. Yet Allende could not afford to repudiate this important bloc of left-wing sentiment. It could even be used at times as a warning to the intransigents on the other side. But it added always to the difficulty of his attempt to move left with the constitutional framework he inherited.

The problems facing Allende as he took office were thus truly formidable. Unable to effect any substantial modification in the armed forces, he had to live with the permanent danger of a reactionary military coup. He was saddled with the high and middle functionaries of the previous regime operating a cumbersome bureaucratic machine ill suited to perform the purposes he sought. His minority support in both houses of Congress would enable his opponents to drown his plans in a swamp of legalisms and parliamentary maneuvers. Nevertheless, he would have to

75

satisfy the aspirations of his followers without delay, regardless of the fact that the country had a low rate of growth, sluggish agriculture and industry, high unemployment and serious inflation. The United States banking institutions and the international institutions controlled by the United States would not help him as they had helped Frei six years earlier. He would not even be able to finance his inherited debts, to say nothing of getting additional credits. How these varied issues were attacked will be the subject of the next chapter.

3.

Law Versus Power

The most urgent tasks the new regime set itself were to complete the land reform begun and then atrophied by the Christian Democrats, and to get control of the banks and major industries which dominated what their program called the social sector of the economy. Among these industries copper held a unique importance as the source of nearly all the country's foreign exchange.

The most straightforward task was land reform. The law passed during the Frei administration gave all the power needed. It provided for expropriation not only of poorly worked estates but also of corporately owned properties and lands under single ownership of over two hundred "basic" acres. The "basic" unit was an acre of good irrigated land near Santiago, and each owner was allowed to retain land to the same value as two hundred such acres. Compensation was set at the value for which the land was assessed for tax purposes. Only ten percent of that value was normally to be paid in cash, the balance in 25-year bonds.

In addition to the law, Allende had the man who knew how to administer it, Jacques Chonchol, 44 years old, one of the world's leading experts on land reform. After studies in London and Paris, Chonchol had observed the beginnings of land reform under Castro in Cuba, as well as Peru's programs. He was working for the Food and Agriculture Organization of the United Nations as overseer of land reform in all Latin America when picked by Frei in 1964 to head the Chilean program. It was he who had drawn up the new law passed in 1967, and he resigned from the Frei government and the Christian Democrats the following year when he could not get the backing he needed to put the provisions of that law into full effect. Chonchol was a man to inspire confidence. Even his political opponents respected him. "He is one of the few politicians in Chile who has precise goals, clear, frank ideas, and the opportunity to express them, the tenacity to realize them, and an absolute consistency in all his actions." That evaluation was offered by conservative Senator Ibáñez in the spring of 1971, when many were blaming Chonchol for the outbreaks of rural violence that followed his first steps to implement the land reform. As Minister of Agriculture for UP, said Ibáñez, "Chonchol is doing exactly the same as he did when vice-president of INDAP [Chile's agricultural development institute], the same as he did in Cuba, the same as he did when a functionary of FAO in charge of preparing land reform for Latin America. He has proceeded with an unobjectionable consistency. No one can feel deceived by the actions of Mr. Chonchol, and he who says he is, is deceived only because he wants to deceive himself. Mr. Chonchol has been clear, and will continue to act in the same manner in which he has always acted."[1]

Because of the mountainous nature of the country and other natural obstacles, less than a seventh of land surface is suitable for agriculture or livestock raising. Most of the 30 million fertile acres are well located, however, in the central valleys close to the major population centers, with the best land still concentrated in the enormous holdings with which the Spanish kings had awarded their favorites. Although there had been substantial changes of ownership, especially during the twentieth century, no change in the type of land holding resulted. Over three quarters of all agricultural land was in big estates which employed more than twelve workers or tenants. On the average estate, only two out of every five arable acres were used productively. The landlord typically drew the bulk of his income from his industrial or commercial activities in the city and from his investments. He rarely put money into the land to raise production. He held it primarily because it gave him social prestige and political power. This power was exercised in the first instance over his tenants, laborers and sharecroppers. Many laborers, known as *inquilinos*, received most of their pay in the form of a small plot of land. The landlord supplied credit at planting time, and he acted as marketing agent for the sale of any produce beyond the needs of the laborer's family. Productivity was high on the land in big estates that was actually used, both because it was the best land to start with, and because the owner's access to capital and credit enabled him to obtain rights to irrigation water, to buy the best seeds and to use the optimum amounts of fertilizers, insecticides, fungicides and labor-saving machinery. But because three-fifths of the land in big estates was left unused, their total contribution to agricultural production fell far short of their proportion of the country's agricultural land. The small and medium-sized farms, highly overworked with 80 to 95 percent of their area under cultivation, and with very little technical or financial help, accounted for 40 percent of total agricultural production on only 21 percent of the arable land.

Chilean agriculture was sluggish even in the 1920s, and it never recovered from the depression of the 1930s. From the time of the Second World War, population grew faster than the production of food. Between 1945 and 1963, food imports rose 205 percent, and food exports dropped 26 percent, so that a quarter of all foreign exchange was spent for food and left the country short of needed intermediate and capital goods. By the early 1960s, Chile was importing 28 percent of its meat, 32 percent of its milk, and 22 percent of its wheat. Imports of food from the United States alone were over $21 million in 1969-70 and over $30 million in 1970-71. By 1954, only a quarter of the work force was employed in agriculture, making Chile one of the most urbanized of Latin American countries. The inefficiency of agriculture, resulting from its undercapitalization and structural distortions, was such that this quarter of the work force was responsible for only 8.5 percent of the gross domestic product. Incomes of the rural population, apart from the big landowners, were miserable, with per capita agricultural income less than half the national average. For the lowest 70 percent of the peasants, even including the value of the home-grown produce consumed, the per capita income was less than a hundred dollars annually. Illiteracy was vastly higher than the official 18 percent. Diets were deficient, housing miserable, and infant mortality high. A third of the labor force was estimated to be economically redundant. And the relationship of these people to the resources available to them grew worse each year. The number of *inquilinos* fell by half between 1955 and 1965, while the area in sharecropping rose, as did the number of landless laborers and the owners of holdings too small to provide minimum levels of living. The flight from the countryside of migrants unprepared for urban living speeded up, the migrants settling in the *callampas*, the "mushroom slums" which in the 1960s became the dominant characteristic not only of Santiago but of every Chilean city.

The prospect of United States aid under the Alliance for Progress had encouraged the Chilean Congress to pass a land reform law under President Jorge Alessandri in 1962, but it proved to be pure window dressing, giving land to only a few thousand applicants. The Frei program was more substantial. By September 1970, the Land Reform Corporation (CORA) had expropriated 1,364 estates with a total area of some 8.5 million acres, of which 700,000 were irrigated, representing 18 percent of Chile's irrigated land and nearly 12 percent of its non-irrigated agricultural land. But this reform sidestepped the most basic issue, that of power. It took the least productive and most under-capitalized land, leaving the good land in the possession of the oligarchs, who quickly moved to strengthen their position by raising production, discharging temporary workers, buying labor-saving machinery, and building a coalition with small farmers and those peasants who benefitted from the first expropriations to oppose more radical land-reform measures.

Instead of working to reduce the power of the big landowners, the Frei reform was actually strengthening them. By eliminating the marginal producers whose land was of poor quality, it was leaving a solid core of prosperous owners. Around them it was creating cooperatives in which privileged peasants would not only themselves work but employ large numbers of migrant workers and of laborers living on subsistence plots. This would result in the creation of a small rural middle class, but without resolving the problems of the lowest class. And thanks to the continued power of the big landowners, they were able to secure for themselves the major benefits of the credit designed to modernize agriculture. A University of Maryland study revealed that between 1965 and 1969 landowners not affected by the reform increased their investments by 120 percent. Investment was concentrated in large part in agricultural machinery which reduced the labor content of production and lessened the dependence on farm laborers. The process was facilitated by investment credits provided by the state. The state bank doubled its credits from an average of $2000 per loan in 1964 to $4000 in 1968, and it tripled the amount dispensed by CORFO, both of these being organizations which catered principally to big landowners. Such organizations as the Land Reform Institute which worked with small farmers and cooperatives had relatively few resources. They had, for example, only 30 percent of the veterinarians and agronomists.[2]

By 1971, accordingly, the old power structures were still standing in the Chilean countryside. But a new power base was in the making. The enactment of a law encouraging the creation of agricultural labor unions in 1967, about the same time as the land reform law, had mobilized the laborers and small farmers. Only 24 unions with a total of 1,658 members existed when that law was passed. By 1970 there were nearly 4,000 organizations, including agricultural unions, committees of small farmers, farmworker cooperatives and resettlements, with a total membership of more than a quarter million. Under the 1967 law, the workers had the right to strike if two-thirds of the members agreed, and the farmer was forbidden to introduce scab labor. A section of the law which would be used extensively by Allende gave the President authority to force the owner to harvest his crops if the process had been interrupted by an illegal strike or a lockout during the harvesting season. The rationale for this provision was that loss of the harvest would hurt not only its owner but the general population.

This new internal dynamism of the peasants, combined with the effective suspension of land reform activities by the Frei regime after 1969, built up to the point of explosion. Cautín province, which has Chile's largest concentration of Indians, the country's densest and poorest rural population, and the highest incidence of rural unemployment, was the center of the disturbances. It is less than a century since the Mapuches were finally subjugated and confined to reservations, and a process of stealing land from these reservations by legal and extra-legal devices has gone on ever since. Militants belonging to the MIR organization had been organizing among peasants and Indians since 1968, and in November 1970 thousands of students from Santiago and Concepción volunteered to spend part of their long summer vacation in the Cautin countryside. Land seizures began almost immediately. Indians moved back fences to return to their reservations land that had been stolen from them. By early 1971, hundreds of farms were being seized each month by groups of peasants.

Often there were internal conflicts, as when the Indians from the neighboring reservation clashed with the *inquilinos* working on a farm for the right to seize it. Newspapers controlled by the rich played on the fears of the middle classes with stories of kidnapped landowners, raped wives, terrorized families, rural chaos and disrupted production. Under a headline screaming that drugged Mapuches were on the war path, *La Prensa* reported that leftist students were giving the Indians little yellow pep pills which were activating their basest instincts. Further south, guerrilla groups began to form along the Argentine border. A leader known as Comandante Pepe who quickly assumed mythical proportions was said to have helped peasants seize more than a million acres by forming them into brigades with a semblance of military discipline.

The challenge to the regime was serious, and Allende's response gave a clue to his intentions. One thing became clear. Unlike former presidents, he would not in a crisis side with the strong against the weak. While pleading with all the means at his disposal for patience, he refused to use force against the peasants. "The Mapuches have been degraded, humiliated and destroyed for generations," he said. "And they are hungry. We cannot expect them to wait until the law expropriates land that was stolen from them decades ago. Men who are hungry often do not wait to reason." Simultaneously, he warned the landowners not to attempt to impose the law of the strong as they had done in the past, but to wait for the government to resolve the issues. "If they attempt violence, they are going to be confronted with the violence that the President of the Republic can unleash against them."[3]

Jacques Chonchol meanwhile pushed ahead with his program under the shower of brickbats from right and left. In the first hundred days of the new regime, spurred by the seizures, he signed expropriation decrees for 130 estates and large farms. By the end of a year, the first stage had been effectively completed with the expropriation of some 1,200 properties. Nearly 14,000 families had been settled on the expropriated land, and it was estimated that it could still accommodate a further 22 thousand.

The main purpose of the land reform had, nevertheless, as yet only begun. Councils of peasants had been set up everywhere, but much still remained to be done in order to make the peasants themselves the dominant force through their organizations in the process of restructuring Chile's rural life. Marketing, supply, processing and credit institutions had to be transformed. The bureaucracy had to be retrained to fit the needs of this new power structure. All of this involved far more than simply nationalizing institutions now privately owned and controlled. Other power relationships would have to change in order to achieve the purpose. The state bank and the state development corporation were in existence for a long time, but their record of help to the peasants was not much better than that of private institutions. And all these additional aspects of the land reform could develop only in step with the other changes being promoted by the UP in Chile.

Of these changes, the one to cause least difficulty within Chile but the most in its international relations was the nationalization of the United States-dominated copper mining industry. By 1970, everybody in Chile was agreed that the Chileanization of copper under Frei had not achieved its objectives. It had meant basically, in the words of Teresa Hayter, who was then working for the Inter-American Development Bank, that "the Chilean government put up most of the capital for expansion." Chile's ownership of 51 percent of the shares gave it no voice in management or policy. During the Vietnam War, the companies sold copper to the United States at prices far below the London market price, and Congress had to pass a new law in 1969 to force them to stop this practice. While Chile's revenue from copper declined, the profits of the companies soared. The companies undertook to double production by 1972 by means of new investment with borrowed capital supplied in part by the Chilean government, in part by loans from the United States Export-Import Bank and other United States financial institutions and guaranteed by the government of Chile. Such borrowed capital to the amount of $579 million was in fact invested between 1966 and 1970, but without any significant growth of production.

Although it was not publicly known until later, the copper companies had been failing to live up to their commitments in additional ways. They were many millions of dollars in arrears on their tax payments. They allowed the mines to fall into a condition of general disrepair. When a French technical consulting firm was retained by the Chilean government in 1971, its engineers reported that the mines were in shocking condition because of neglect, mismanagement and corporate irresponsibility. The situation was particularly bad in Anaconda's Chuquicamata. New installations had been badly built with inferior materials. Roads were badly planned, and adequate water supplies had not been provided. Equipment had been negligently installed and maintained. Working conditions were unsafe and unhygienic. Future production had been sabotaged by such practices as bulldozing earth on top of deposits not yet mined. Facilities for training Chilean technicians either did not exist or were inferior. This French report was subsequently confirmed by a team of Soviet engineers. [4]

Even if not all these facts were known, there was enough information on the record to convince all segments of Chilean opinion that the only solution of their long conflict with the foreign companies was to nationalize the mines. The Christian Democrats had themselves reached this conclusion by 1969 and included nationalization in their election program in 1970. The National Party was less enthusiastic but decided to accept the clear expression of the national will. Allende, nevertheless, moved with extreme circumspection. He knew he was exposing Chile to the wrath of the world's most powerful business magnates, and that they would have on their side the diplomatic and economic clout of the United States government, in addition to their own vast resources. He decided, accordingly, to give his action the greatest possible solemnity as well as the clearest possible juridic justification by means of an amendment to the Chilean constitution.

The amendment was unanimously approved by the Chilean Congress on July 16, 1971, in accordance with constitutional amendment procedures which require a two-thirds affirmative vote of Congress. It stated that the country's resources of copper were the property of Chile and it authorized the government to assume formal public ownership of all minerals in the nation's subsoil and to take operational control of the Anaconda, Kennecott and Cerro mines. It stipulated that no compensation was due for minerals as yet unmined, on the ground that under Chilean law all unexploited natural resources were the property of the nation. Compensation was to be paid for installations on the basis of their value as declared in the books of the companies, subject to specified deductions. The possible deductions fell into two general categories. Any costs that might be incurred by Chile to correct defects in the property caused by neglect, mismanagement or sabotage should be debited against the companies. And any profits already realized beyond a reasonable level should similarly be debited. This concept of unreasonable or excessive profits goes back to a Chilean law of 1955 which gave the government the right to determine a fair rate of return on the investments of foreign capital that can be repatriated as profits. The President of the Republic was empowered to determine the exact level of fair profit, and the formula finally worked out fixed the rate at 12 percent of invested capital. The law further specified that capital remittances abroad by the companies during the 40 years of operations be deducted from the net investment, since these in fact represented a return of capital. The government calculated that the amounts so withdrawn totalled $500 million.[5]

One of the most widely recognized principles of national law and most fully accepted principles of international law is the right of the state, known in legal language as eminent domain, to take possession of any property within the boundaries of the state for reasons judged by the state itself to be in the public interest. The right is recognized in the Fifth Amendment to the Constitution of the United States and in the Declaration of the Rights of Man proclaimed in 1789 by the French Revolution. Recent applications of this principle include nationalization of oil by Mexico in 1938 and by Iran in 1951, and nationalization of coal, electricity, gas and transport by Great Britain and France between 1945 and 1950.

The right of the property owner to compensation is less clear as a matter of law. The United States is bound by its own constitution not to take private property for public use without just compensation. The Permanent Court of Arbitration (Hague Tribunal) ruled in 1925 in *Norway versus the United States* that the United States had to pay "a fair compensation" to Norwegian citizens whose property rights it had seized during the First World War. The court itself decided what constituted a fair compensation in the case. Other cases heard by the court stress that it is the right of every sovereign state to determine its own political, economic and social future, and that "if need or theory require that the ownership of property should be vested in the state, its freedom of action should not be fettered by the fact that it is too poor to pay the fair market price for alien property."[6] This means that the foreign investor must include the possibility of nationalization among the risks of doing business, just as the investor must who does business in his own country. Historically, the communist countries have paid little compensation for nationalized property, but "in noncommunist countries it has been common practice to compensate the owners of nationalized properties, at least in part."[7] United States and other investors settled with Mexico in 1947 for less than a third of the value they had placed on their oil holdings.

The fact that a country had made a concession to a foreign company does not prevent it from later nationalizing the property subject to the concession. The existence of this power is implicit in the provision of section 10 of the first article of the United States Constitution which forbids states of the Union—but not the United States itself—to make any law "impairing the obligation of contracts." It was established explicitly by the Hague Tribunal in the Anglo-Iranian Oil Company dispute in 1952. The Court there ruled that a concession made by a state to a foreign corporation is not an international agreement and is subject to the law of the conceding state. The same principle is stated in a resolution dealing with "the inalienable right of all countries to exercise permanent sovereignty over their natural resources in the interest of their national development," passed by the General Assembly of the United Nations at its 21st session. That resolution "confirms that the exploitation of natural resources in each country shall always be conducted in accordance with its national laws and regulations."

The calculation of the indemnity for Chile's national-ized mining properties was the responsibility of the Comptroller General, whose office under the Chilean constitutional system is a separate and independent fourth institutional branch of government, charged with verifying and overseeings all public receipts and expenditures. The Comptroller holds office for twelve years, and the present holder had been named by the Christian Democrats before UP came to power. He was totally unsympathetic to the UP program and would subsequently be a major problem for Allende. It was he who determined that the book value of the copper properties was $629 million, and that the companies had already taken $775 million in excess profits out of the country, leaving them in debt to Chile, to the extent of $145 million. Even the head of the Catholic Church in Chile, Cardinal Raúl Silva Henríquez, a middle-of-the-road churchman who always had identified with the Christian Democrats, had only praise for the procedures used by the Allende regime. "The process of nationalization has been constitutionally impeccable," he commented. "With the respect for the law that is traditional in Chile, the principle consecrated by the United Nations that every country has the right to reclaim its basic resources has been put into practice. It is not proper that this matter be presented in unfriendly terms between two governments and much less between two peoples."[8]

One point left unclear by the constitutional amendment was Chile's obligation for the debts incurred by the companies in the expansion program, debts which the Chilean government had guaranteed. Chile tried at first to offset these debts against the overpayments. When Kennecott got a court order in New York blocking the bank accounts of fourteen Chilean agencies in the United States, Chile paid a first installment of $5.8 million on notes held by Kennecott in a total amount of $92.7 million. Allende further indicated that, in his concern to remain strictly within his legal rights and not to press any doubtful claims, he would probably assume all these disputed debts.

The Chileans knew in advance that the United States reaction would be negative. President Nixon had ranged himself on the side of wealth and power when he failed to send the customary message of greeting to President Allende on his election. He had followed up with what *The New York Times* described editorially as a "boorish rebuff"[9] by breaking the protocol traditions and declining Allende's invitation to an United States warship off the Chilean coast to visit a Chilean port. At the diplomatic level, he had been even more explicit, officially cautioning the Chilean government early in 1971 that its plans for nationalizing copper could seriously damage relations with the United States.[10]

In his State of the World Message, February 25, 1971, Nixon formulated an arm's length relationship with the Allende regime in terms that suggested an iron fist rather than a velvet glove at the end of that arm. The United States, he said, would have with the government of Chile "the kind of relationship it is prepared to have with us." Throughout the year, and with increasing harshness as Allende went ahead with his programs, he evolved a policy which was formalized in his "Policy Statement, Economic Assistance and Investment Security in Developing Nations." Without mentioning Chile by name, it spelled out what it could expect: "When a country expropriates a significant United States interest without making reasonable provision for such compensation to United States citizens, we will presume that the United States will not extend new bilateral economic benefits to the expropriating country unless and until it is determined that the country is taking reasonable steps to provide adequate compensation or that there are major factors affecting United States interests which require continuance of all or part of these benefits. In the face of the expropriatory circumstances just described, we will presume that the United States government will withhold its support from loans under consideration in multilateral development banks."

Anaconda and Kennecott were, accordingly, assured of massive backing when they announced their intention to fight the Chilean decision as what they both called its violation of international law. Secretary of State Rogers had already undertaken to use economic pressures at a meeting with executives of the Bank of America, First National City Bank, ITT, Ford, Anaconda, and Ralston Purina behind closed doors in October 1971. "The Nixon administration is a business administration," he assured them. "Its mission is to protect American business." Accordingly, it would cut off aid unless Chile gave "prompt compensation." Asked by some of the executives if such a hard line might not be interpreted as "a slap in the face" to Chile and other Latin American nations, he replied that "such measures might be the only language they understand."[11]

Not all the United States companies in Chile had been ready to go along with the CIA plan to promote economic chaos in Chile. The weight of evidence available from the ITT papers and other sources indicates that Anaconda helped finance a campaign of disruption before the election, and that it also joined with Kennecott in what was effectively sabotage in the copper mines. Ralston Purina cut back production sharply. NIBSA, the leading producer of brass valves and other fittings, a subsidiary of Northern Indiana Brass Company, shut down its plant and laid off 280 workers the day before Allende's inauguration. A representative of the parent company, Northern Indiana Brass, was accused of suggesting an "Indonesian solution" (killing all communists) for Chile. Purina, a subsidiary of Ralston Purina and the country's largest producer of animal feed, also cut production back sharply.[11]

Other United States firms, however, were apparently unwilling in 1970 to embark on programs of sabotage or disruption. They included General Motors, Ford and the Bank of America. Within the United States government there was a similar difference of opinion. Treasury Secretary John Connally and John Petty, his assistant, supported CIA's Broe in his hard line, while Assistant Secretary of State for Latin American Affairs Charles Meyer and Henry Kissinger favored a lower profile. But, as it soon became clear, the difference concerned tactics, not objectives. The low-profile group was convinced that Allende would either return of his own accord to support of the system as soon as he was securely in office, as all previous presidents had done, or that the financial pressures they could exert would suffice to destroy him.

The arguments in favor of this approach were serious. Allende had inherited a foreign debt contracted by his predecessors amounting to $3 billion, one of the highest per capita debts in the world, especially when related to Chile's gross national product. The United States had been willing to allow this debt to grow during the 1960s because of its contribution to the export of goods made in the United States, and because of Washington's desire to support a friendly government and simultaneously to maintain leverage over it. Chilean governments had been willing to accept the dependency created by such indebtedness, fearing the pressures that they would suffer at home from the wealthy groups who constituted their power base, if they insisted on the structural changes that would be necessary to raise the level of internal development. According to a 1966 study of aid to Chile made by the United States

Senate, foreign credit had in recent years financed as much as 40 percent of official investment.[12]

When Frei became president in 1964, service on this debt had already grown so heavy that it would absorb 40 percent of all earnings of foreign exchange derived from exports of copper. Frei accordingly renegotiated this debt, then proceeded to borrow more heavily than before in the hope that new investments would generate additional resources and ultimately enable the country to pay off its obligations. US-AID was anxious to strengthen the Frei regime, which it regarded as the most friendly it could hope to get in Chile, and in 1965-66 it was financing 14 percent of the entire Chilean budget. Even with the renegotiation of the old loans, the level of new ones was so high that up to 30 percent of available foreign exchange went to servicing of debts during Frei's six years in office. The one thing that prevented a crisis was a rapid rise in the price of copper, from 29 cents a pound in the early 1960s to 66 cents in 1969.[13] It enabled the country to build up its foreign exchange reserves to $387 million in July 1970. Against this balance was a debt of $3 billion, of which $300 million was due for repayment in 1971, $400 million in 1972, and a further $400 million in 1973. To add to the pressures on Allende, the world price of copper fell precipitately from the 74 cents a pound record price registered in the first half of 1970 to 52 cents by October. Whether this was coincidental or the result of manipulation designed to embarrass Allende has never been established. Charges of an "international plot" to undermine copper prices were made to the press by spokesmen for the Chilean government, but the facts were never fully unearthed.[14] Whatever the reasons, it was perfectly obvious that Allende could not hope to meet his debt obligations without a further renegotiation of the debts he had inherited.

Allende was fully aware of all these threats when he took office. Nevertheless, he decided to move ahead with his commitment to take over those industries and activities which he believed the national interest required to be controlled by the state, while careful at the same time to remain strictly within the law. The campaign of disruption in which some firms engaged played into his hands. Legislation passed in the 1930s provided for state intervention in and temporary administration of factories not meeting the production norms fixed by the government. It was now invoked against the firms which arbitrarily cut back production. The first firms to come under state management in virtue of this law were a textile firm owned jointly by the Yarur interests and W.R. Grace, NIBSA and Purina. Several Anaconda and Kennecott activities were similarly "intervened," even before their nationalization by constitutional amendment. Another major intervention was that of the Ford plant, occupied by the workers in May 1971, after the company announced the laying off of 400 of the 600 workers.

Control of other companies was secured by negotiation or by purchase of stock in the open market. Allende announced in January 1971 that he was sending a bill to Congress to nationalize banking. But he was ready to buy out immediately at a price higher than the market those shareholders who were willing to sell, and they would be paid in bonds that would be adjusted upward with change in the cost of living. Compensation under the proposed law, he warned, would be less, and in bonds not adjustable for cost-of-living changes. The Central Bank began immediately to buy stock in private banks, and within eight months had a controlling interest in 19 of the country's 22 private commercial banks. Those who had previously had a monopoly of stock market transactions protested volubly at the unfair state competition. The country's biggest publishing company, Zig-Zag, was acquired by stock purchase in February 1971, when it was on the verge of bankruptcy, having failed to pay its 900 workers for eight weeks. Other firms were acquired by agreement. In March 1971, Bethlehem-Chile Iron Mines, a subsidiary of Bethlehem Steel, sold its shares to Acero del Pacifico, Chile's largest steel producer, and the state bought the 45 percent of Acero del Pacifico stock in private hands for $90.6 million payable over three to eight years, thus acquiring total ownership. The state also bought the remaining controlling stock in the country's major nitrate and iodine producer from the United States owned Anglo-Lautaro corporation. The first company in the "mixed" sector as defined in the UP program resulted from an agreement with RCA, which sold Chile 51 percent of its subsidiary, the largest Chilean manufacturer of radio equipment.

Legal though all these steps undoubtedly were, they collectively constituted a confirmation of the worst fears of the foreign firms doing business in Chile. If Allende completed the UP economic program, as he obviously intended to do, their control of decision making in Chile would be ended, and their prospects of future business in the "mixed" sector would not only be relatively slim but always subject to Chile's majority ownership and control. The principles already enunciated made it further clear that Chile's formula for compensation to the companies still to be taken over was far removed from the idea these companies held of the value of their properties in Chile. In consequence, as the year 1971 progressed, the United States government and companies drew closer together, facing Chile with a policy that became steadily more hostile.

Total United States government loans to Chile between 1946 and 1970 were $1.4 billion, of which $954 million was outstanding in 1970. During that period, Chile borrowed a further $566 million from international organizations dominated by the United States, almost all of it from the World Bank and the Inter-American Development Bank. US-AID help was particularly high during the Frei presidency, peaking at $269 million in 1967. It stopped suddenly when Allende was elected, the Export-Import Bank reacting to the news by dropping Chile to its lowest credit category. The first application of the Allende regime for credit was in early 1971 when it asked the Eximbank for a series of loans totalling nearly $200 million, of which the most urgent item was $21 million to buy three Boeing jets for use by the state-owned LAN-Chile on its routes to Europe. All the other aircraft used by the company were Boeings, similarly financed by the Eximbank, and buying from another company would involve the cost of new training for flight and ground crews, stockpiling of additional parts, and building of expensive maintenance facilities. After a delay of six months, the bank notified Chile that no loans or guarantees of loans made by private banks would be forthcoming until the question of compensation for United States mining and other interests in Chile had been resolved. United States officials had admitted during the negotiations that Chile had been scrupulous in paying debts, and that the issue was not creditworthiness but the political situation. The decision was reportedly made on the White House level, probably by Kissinger's "Chile Task Force." When Chile turned to Britain for VC-10s as being the next most suitable aircraft, it was informed that they were "not available," presumably also a political decision made under pressure from Washington and calculated to warn Chile that Western capitalism was going to stand together in support of property rights as determined by it. Chile had then no choice but to turn to Russia for Ilyushins, using a line of credit already offered by the Soviet Union.[15]

Even publications in the United States and Chile which were notoriously unsympathetic to Allende joined with his many sympathizers in Latin America in denouncing this "big stick" policy, which was identified as the declaration of war by Washington and its assertion that it was going to rely on its naked power to force Chile to submit to its version of legality. *El Mercurio* of Santiago, Allende's bitter enemy, said it was a blow against normal relations with the United States. *The Miami Herald* called it editorially "a disaster in search of an opportunity to happen," and *The Washington Post* concurred in an editorial titled "Bullying Chile." It said the action represented "a major failure of American policy," adding that "no self-respecting government, marxist or otherwise, can be expected to dance a jig for Henry Kearns—who is president of Exim."[16] Other United States newspapers concurred.

Washington's policy extended not only to refusal of new loans but even to stopping the disbursement of loans granted earlier. The Eximbank's further suspension of its guarantee and insurance program for private loans to Chile served as a cue to commercial banks. The big banks closely tied to the copper companies, Chase Manhattan, Chemical, First National City, Manufacturers Hanover and Morgan Guarantee, cut off all credits. Other banks cut back sharply, reducing the $220 million in short-term credit lines previously available to $35 million.

The World Bank, although formally an agency of the United Nations, is in fact controlled by the United States. Robert S. McNamara, its president since 1968, was United States Secretary of Defense during the previous seven years, and before that a top official of the Ford Motor Company. Up to Allende's election it had lent Chile $235 million, but it refused every subsequent request, including a loan sought for a fruit-growing project, the second stage of a cattle breeding project which had been started with a World Bank loan under Frei, and an ongoing electrification program which the Bank had been actively assisting for 20 years. Its stated reason for refusing further financing of the electrification program was that the rates set under Allende's worker-oriented policies were too low. McNamara even went further. In an unusual departure from banker

97

diplomacy, he made statements calculated to damage Chile's credit. "The primary condition for banking lending—a soundly managed economy with a clear potential for utilizing additional funds—has not been met. The Chilean economy is in severe difficulty."[17] The charter of the World Bank, which has the status of an international treaty or agreement, specifically commits the members not to use their voting power or influence with the Bank as a tool to bring pressure on a country with which they have a bilateral conflict.

The Inter-American Development Bank had been even more generous to Chile in the past than the World Bank, lending a total of $310 million between 1959 and 1970. In 1971 a mission from the Bank visited Chile and reached agreement with the Chilean authorities on a petrochemical complex, precisely the kind of activity the bank was created to foster, involving the transfer of technology and the capability of earning foreign exchange. The loan was, nevertheless, refused, as were applications for loans for electric power and gas liquefaction. Although the economic situation had not perceptibly changed, Chile had suddenly become "economically unstable," "uncreditworthy," and in "unfavorable exchange position," all this in spite of Chile's perfect record of repayment, a record that continued under Allende even when no new loans were forthcoming. A member of the bank's staff expressed the frustration shared by many when he commented: "The Inter-American Development Bank is behaving like an umbrella that's up only when it's not raining."[18]

The IADB did make one significant exception to its refusal of loans. It gave a $7 million loan to the Catholic University, and a $4.6 million loan to the Austral University located in the predominantly German-speaking and conservative south of the country. These two universities had large and influential groups opposed to the UP policies and program, groups which it was in the United States interest to encourage.

US-AID itself similarly made some curious exceptions to its boycott. While the "food for peace" program valued at $4.3 million in 1970 was stopped, this just as Allende had guaranteed that every Chilean child would get a daily glass of milk, a "technical assistance" program to train "selected Chileans" in urban administration, rural development, exchange of labor officials, and some "small-scale self-help projects," was continued. This exception enabled the United States to keep its AID staffs in Chile and to promote within Chile interests and activities calculated to strengthen the anti-Allende forces. Visits to the United States by labor leaders and organizers, for example, were conducted by the American Institute of Free Labor Development (AIFLD), an organization funded by United States business, trade unions and government, and frequently identified by Latin Americans as a front for the CIA. In Chile, its help reportedly was concentrated during Allende's presidency on maritime, professional and airline unions which were actively involved in efforts to cause economic, social and political disruption.[19]

The other exception to the AID boycott was in favor of Chile's armed forces. They had long been the privileged beneficiaries of the Pentagon's concern and material support. When the United States Military Assistance Program began in 1952, Chile quickly became one of the prime recipients of military aid on the continent. Between 1950 and 1965, more than 2,000 Chileans received training in the United States as part of this program, more than any other Latin American country with the exception of Brazil and Peru. Chile received the highest per capita amount of military aid in Latin America between 1953 and 1966, and the flow continued at the same level in the following years, bringing the grand total to $144 million by 1970. The largesse continued after Allende took office, nearly $6 million in 1971, over $12 million in 1972, and a similar amount projected for 1973. The reason for this courting of the armed forces would later become clear.[20]

4.

Bread and Work

When the Allende administration took office in November 1970, the broad outlines of the opposition strategy and objective were already clear. The objective was to get rid of Allende before he could carry out the radical structural changes he had promised. Some of his opponents were already committed to violence, concentrating their attacks on the homes of wealthy people, banks and similar targets, in the hope that such attacks would be blamed on the militant left and bring a backlash. One such plan backfired seriously, a plot to kidnap General René Schneider, the commander-in-chief of the armed forces. He resisted and was killed. Two attempts were made on Allende's life, and—as he said himself—"they were not successful because of the devotion and zeal of my personal guard of revolutionary comrades."

Most members of the opposition, however, were not yet ready for violence. Chile prided itself on a long tradition of peaceful political give-and-take. Unlike the United States, it was not in the habit of assassinating its presidents. Indeed, the fatal wounding of Schneider was the first

101

assassination attempt, successful or otherwise, against a high Chilean official in 140 years.[1] In addition, there was a general consensus that the objective could be achieved by a lower-profile strategy, namely, by the creation of economic chaos with the cooperation of the United States companies which controlled vital segments of the economy.

One component in the strategy was to encourage skilled workers and professionals to leave the country with their money. Malcolm Browne reported from Argentina in September 1970 to *The New York Times* that hotels in Buenos Aires were full and those in Mendoza even more crowded, with the number of migrant families estimated in the tens of thousands. He quoted a financial expert as believing that "most of the really wealthy Chileans had gotten their money out of Chile a long time ago, at least before the election. What we're seeing now is a flood of the smaller fish who have suddenly decided they may be wiped out."[2] Next it was the turn of the mining companies to strip the mines of engineers and managers, giving them big separation benefits and offering jobs elsewhere. This was done so openly that *El Mercurio* ran advertisements in English saying that "qualified technicians are wanted in well-paid jobs abroad."[3]

Objectively, the UP program did not threaten the interests of the *petite bourgeoisie*, truck owners, shopkeepers, professionals and white-collar workers. On the contrary, the major expansion of purchasing power which would follow the rational exploitation of the vast areas of arable land hitherto held idle and full utilization of the substantial unused margin of installed industrial capacity would quickly benefit these sectors. Nothing less than economic chaos would threaten the interests of these key sectors of society, and that was why it had to be pursued by all means, fair and foul. In consequence, the big landowners slaughtered their cattle and left their fields unplanted. Big business suspended new investments, putting its money into speculation and hoarding, quickly building a black market which insulated them from the government's programs for equitable distribution of food and other basic products. Panic buying stimulated by the communications media created shortages where none existed. *El Mercurio* had only to report a shortage of tooth paste to produce a buying wave that took every tube off store shelves. The very wealthy could afford the black market prices. The middle sectors were the ones who felt the pinch.

Given its commitment to function within the constitution and the laws, the weapons available to the UP coalition to fight such strategies were limited. The Christian Democrats began to pull away from the UP almost immediately after throwing their vote to Allende to confirm him as president. Apart from the nationalization of copper, there was no hope of cooperation from Congress. In addition, part of the election deal was a law to give job stability to the civil servants appointed by the Frei administration. Allende would have to function as best he could with a civil service dominated by his opponents.

It was absolutely essential, nevertheless, to demonstrate in concrete ways to the elements in society which formed the natural constituency of the UP coalition that things had changed in their favor. Vigorous pursuit of land reform and the nationalization of essential industries gave a certain emotional satisfaction, but right away bread was needed on the table. Chile's production of goods and services represented a per capita income of about $600 a year, which placed it quite high among Latin American countries, but the distribution of this income was grossly unequal. The top five percent of the population monopolized 27 percent of it, while the bottom 50 percent had to make do with 17 percent, and the bottom 20 percent with less than four percent. That meant that the weekly expenditure on food, clothing and shelter of one Chilean in five was $2.30 or less. In Greater Santiago, in which a third of the population was concentrated, 21 percent of the work force was unemployed.[4]

Allende used the standard methods of applied political science to correct this condition rapidly. When the military dictatorship came to power in Brazil in 1964, it adjusted prices and wages, manipulated credit and diverted investment so as to cut the purchasing power of the worker to 64 percent of what it was previously and transfer a far higher proportion of the benefits of the economy to the small wealthy sector and its foreign associates. Similarly, President Nixon in the United States used controls over wages, prices, credit and investment to increase company profits at the expense of workers. Allende did the same thing in reverse. He stimulated demand, with a corresponding favorable impact on production and employment, by a sharp increase in money wages combined with a price freeze, thus utilizing the unused capacity of industry. The lowest wages were raised more than the higher levels, and in state-controlled industry a ceiling of 20 times the income of the average worker was established as the top salary of the highest paid administrator. Family allowances for blue-collar and white-collar workers were equalized, and an undertaking was given that those for rural workers would be brought in line with those for urban workers within a year. Daily pints of milk were delivered free to pregnant mothers, nursing mothers and every child under the age of fifteen. This was a particularly significant measure. Half of the children in Chile under 15 years were undernourished, and 600,000 were mentally retarded through lack of protein, especially during the first months of life. Bus fares were reduced and equalized. Utility rates were frozen, as were also the rents in public housing. When industries attempted to cut production on the plea that the price freeze made operation unprofitable, they were taken over under the law of 1932 which authorized state intervention in an enterprise that failed to fulfil established production quotas.[5]

The most dramatic progress was registered in the area of medical services, Allende's professional interest and most personal concern. In spite of a serious shortage of doctors, estimated at 4,800 in relation to the real needs of the people, a major expansion was effected immediately by giving priority to community clinics over hospitals, by using medical students and paramedics, and by developing preventive medicine campaigns among the poor. Consultations increased by three million in 1971 over the 1970 figures. Infant mortality registered an 11 percent decrease, and fatal diarrhea in children a 20 percent decrease. Deaths from bronchial pneumonia were down 15 percent, and child malnutrition cases seven percent. And with the expanded attention came new attitudes. "The doctors make me feel like a person now," said Alicia Gregua who lives in the Santiago slum of Nogales. The Nogales clinic tripled the hours of medical service in two years, and pediatric visits jumped from 14,000 to 34,000.[6]

The Allende government was as fully aware as the most conventional economists that redistribution of income cannot get very far unless productivity simultaneously rises. On the contrary, the increased purchasing power of the poor will quickly be dissipated in higher prices if enough of the things they need are not available. That became evident in Chile when the rich utilized some of their idle wealth to accumulate hoards of foodstuffs and other supplies. The government replied immediately by creating a state-controlled distribution network to provide food and consumer goods at low prices in all workingclass areas and increased substantially the importation of foodstuffs to satisfy the increased demand.

The first effects of these policies were seen in the municipal elections of April 1971. Both sides approached the elections as they would a plebiscite for or against the UP program. Frei as head of the Christian Democrats joined in a campaign developed by the right-wing media seeking to redefine the concepts of legality and illegality. Legality applied to every action designed to protect the status quo, with emphasis on the "democratic" nature of the opposition to UP and on the "totalitarian" character of the elements united in the UP coalition which encouraged the assumption that any measure the UP proposed or sponsored was probably "illegal." Just three days before the elections, Frei broke his five-month political silence to charge that Allende was leading Chile to "anarchy, violence . . . and an imported image" of totalitarianism.[7] Allende was equally specific about where he stood. "I am not the president of all Chileans," he said in a speech not long before the elections. "I am not the compañero presidente of moneychangers, of the large landowners, of those who have denied land to the workers; I cannot be a companion to speculators. . . . I am not the compañero presidente of those economic clans who have lived by exploiting Chile. I am the president of those who live by their labor and those who put the national interest before their private interests."[8]

For the first time, those aged 18 to 21 were entitled to vote, and although only 112,000 of an estimated 700,000 in this group actually registered, they swelled the voter rolls to a record 3,792,682. When the votes were counted, they reflected exactly the UP prediction that the coalition would raise its proportion to exceed that of the now united opposition. UP candidates received 49.73 percent of the votes cast, to 48.05 percent for the candidates of the Christian Democrats and the National Party. The remaining 2.22 percent represented spoiled votes and votes cast for independents.[9]

Two events shortly after the elections added significantly to the popular base of the UP, a statement from what came to be known as the Group of Eighty Priests, and a new split in the Christian Democrats. Identifying themselves as "living and laboring with the working class," the Group of Eighty ranged themselves solidly with the UP in its commitment to build socialism in Chile, arguing that nothing less could end the exploitation from which their people suffered. Gonzalo Arroyo, a young and highly respected Jesuit, was identified as the group's secretary general. More than half the members were foreigners, as are more than half the priests in Chile.

"Socialism, characterized by the corporate ownership of the means of production, opens the way to a new economy which makes possible an autonomous and accelerated rate of development, as well as the breaking down of societal barriers. However, socialism doesn't only imply a new economy. It must also generate new values, values which will lead to the emergence of a more unified and fraternal society in which workers assume their role with dignity. . . .

"As Christians, we see no incompatibility between Christianity and socialism. On the contrary, as the Cardinal of Santiago said last November, 'there are more evangelical values in socialism than in capitalism.' It is a fact that socialism conveys the hope that man can fulfil himself better, and for that reason fulfill the Gospel better. That makes him more like Jesus Christ, who came to liberate us from all forms of slavery.

"In this sense, we need to eliminate all prejudice and the lack of trust that exists between Christians and Marxists. To the Marxists we say that true religion is not the opiate of the people. On the contrary, it is a liberating stimulus for the constant renewal of the world. And we should remind all Christians that our God is committed to the history of mankind, and that in these days to love one's neighbor means basically to struggle so that this world might be reshaped to approximate as closely as possible the future world for which we all hope and which even now we are in the process of constructing. . . .

"Collaboration will be facilitated, on the one hand, to the degree that marxism is viewed as an instrument of analysis and transformation of society, and on the other, to the degree that we Christians continue purging our faith of all those elements that keep us from making a firm and effective commitment to our society. Therefore, we support the measures that tend toward the social ownership of the means of production, the socialization of banks and monopolistic industries, the acceleration and expansion of the land reform program, etc."[10]

The impact of this statement was heightened by an open letter of support from twelve professors of theology in the Catholic University of Chile. Recalling the statements about "institutionalized violence" made by the bishops of Latin America at Medellin in 1968, they said that the exploitation of Chilean workers was "a result of the dependent capitalist system which exists in Chile," imposing on all Christians an obligation "to identify with the oppressed." Furthermore, "class struggle is not a mere idea but the most cruel reality. To ignore this struggle would be to justify the present situation of misery and injustice. We accept this reality in order to modify it with a love that, transformed into political power, frees the poor and the rich and brings closer the day when the anguished cry of those who suffer will no longer be heard."[11]

This strong commitment to the program of UP, including the marxist socialism with its stress on class struggle to which the major members of the coalition were committed, undoubtedly influenced the outcome of a debate then going on within the Christian Democrats. As Frei led the party ever closer to formal opposition and a coalition with the National Party, some of the younger members became restive. A by-election in July provided the occasion for a showdown. These critics called for a formal

declaration that the party would not under any circumstances form a front with the conservatives, and when their
motion was rejected, they withdrew. The dissidents, including eight deputies, formed their own party, the Movement of the Christian Left (MIC), which from its inception
supported the policies of the UP. Jacques Chonchol, minister of agriculture in the UP coalition, left MAPU with
three other deputies to join the MIC, whose more moderate socialism he regarded as closer to his personal views.
After some hesitation, Allende confirmed him in his ministerial post.

Yet another boost to the UP government was an open
letter to President Nixon signed by 79 Catholic and Protestant missionaries working in Chile, urging him not to
interfere. "We are disappointed and concerned by the
generally negative reaction of the United States," they
wrote. "The great majority of Chileans advocate change
within the law and through the democratic process. . . .
Judge the Chilean experiment in terms of human needs
and aspirations."[12]! Originally called the Missioners' Committee on International Awareness, this group later incorporated lay members and changed its name to Project for
Awareness and Action: United States Christians in Chile
(PARA).

It was a small but highly selective group of sociologists,
political scientists, social workers and people with special-
izations in such disciplines as communications. In early
1973 it counted 23 active members, of whom four worked
half to full time for it, and three more nearly half time. Six
members were priests or ministers, two were nuns and
fifteen were lay people. Seventeen of them were Catholics,
five Methodists and one Reformed Church. Because of the
quality of the members and their strategic distribution in
all parts of Chile and among all sectors of the population,
it became one of the most reliable and authoritative sources of information on developments in Chile.

In spite of such gains for the UP coalition, the two forces remained delicately balanced throughout 1971. A by-election in southern Chile to fill the seat held by Allende before he became president was won by a Socialist with just over 50 percent of the vote. But in Valparaiso, in another by-election, the Socialist candadate lost by one percentage point. In important elections at the University of Chile for the governing council and the post of rector, the Christian Democrat candidate for rector won 51.42 percent of the vote, while the UP won 53 seats on the council to 47 for the opposition.

A point of bitter contention from the very outset was the determination of the government to involve the masses actively in the political process. "We must have authentic participation of the workers not only in politics but also in the social and economic fields," Allende said in February 1971, repeating a familiar theme. "We have set up the national farmers' council. From now on, peasants will play an active part in the study and development of agricultural projects." The opposition concentrated all its efforts to prevent the realization of this program, and that for obvious reasons. In a country in which the have-nots vastly outnumber the haves, the party of the have-nots is assured of a permanent majority if it can mobilize its entire constituency and make the members conscious of their class interests. Traditionally in Chile, the solid core of support for the parties of the Left was in the industrial and urban proletariat which had long been organized into labor unions. The classical proletariat of this type is bigger and more organized in Chile than in most Latin American countries, but it is still a minority of the population. The countryside, in which 30 percent of the population lives, was overwhelmingly anti-UP, in spite of substantial changes in recent years. While the National Party had lost ground with rural voters, the main beneficiary was the Christian Democratic Party. And the new force repre-

110

sented by the shantytowns, while definitely pro-UP or pro-MIR to the extent that it was tapped, was still for the most part unmobilized.

One of the areas in which this conflict—simultaneously philosophical and political—boiled up was in relation to the exercise of justice. Allende early in his term amnestied two groups of young men imprisoned during the previous regime for robbing banks. Both had been altruistically motivated, one group needing the money for a slum building project, the other to promote the purposes of their left-wing organization. He did not approve of what they had done, Allende said, but he thought jail was overreaction when the money was taken in desperation from institutions which lent only to the rich and put their profits in foreign corporations. It was, in his view, a much smaller crime than the complex financial arrangements which robbed the country of millions of dollars at a critical moment after a socialist regime had come to power.

Such decisions and statements brought out the most bitter denunciations of the press as evidence of a government plot to stir up violence and encourage militants to kill all the decent people. One way in which the opposition took its revenge was by rejecting a bill presented in Congress which would have created neighborhood courts. This was a project long urged by Allende. He knew that the poor had no confidence in the law courts to which they were summoned only to be given decisions in which they had no participation and the reasons for which they did not understand. In neighborhood courts with authority to deal with the normal neighborhood issues—drunkenness, wife beating, petty thieving—the people would develop simultaneously respect for law and a sense of constituting a community. For the opposition, such developments represented the creation of power centers over which they could not exercise social control. When slum settlements created their own community structures, including police

111

forces and courts, they reacted with paranoiac vehemence. Their newspapers, highly visible everywhere on news stands, charged that terror was stalking the streets and that the government was encouraging thugs and assassins to intimidate the citizens.

The control of the media of information by the opposition was perhaps the biggest of the structural distortions in Chile which could not be dealt with effectively within the limitations imposed by governing within the law. The UP regime never overcame it. Even the most justified interference with a newspaper, as when in January 1971 the government moved to make *El Mercurio* pay up $380,000 arrears of taxes due since the previous October, brought anguished cries of persecution and warnings that press freedom was imperilled. *El Mercurio*, published in Santiago, Valparaiso and Antofagasta, is Chile's biggest and most influential newspaper, with a daily circulation of 145,000 and 230,000 on Sunday. It supported the National Party and was (and is) frankly slanted in favor of that party in its presentation of the news, as was *La Nacion* in its support of the UP and *La Prensa* in support of the Christian Democrats. Indeed, it was always necessary to read all three of these newspapers in order to know what was happening. And further enlightenment as regards views, if not as regards facts, could be obtained by reading MIR's *El Rebelde* on the far left and *Portada*, the mouthpiece of the extreme Right.

Chile had always a multiplicity of voices, but the disparity in the loudness of the various voices was extreme. A study published shortly before the change of government[13] showed that three business organizations—*El Mercurio*, SOSEPUR and CIPESA—controlled 65 percent of Chile's newspaper publications; and that two groups—Zig-Zag and the Edwards interests which also owned *El Mercurio*—monopolized almost 98 percent of magazines. The purchase of Zig-Zag by the state from the Christian Democrats, who had themselves bought it while in power, helped to redress this condition, but the imbalance was never fully corrected. In 1973 the opposition still owned six Santiago dailies with a combined weekday circulation of 541,000 copies, while pro-government groups and parties had five Santiago dailies with a circulation of 312,000. The opposition press was far more widely distributed in the provinces than the pro-government press.[14]

Even before UP came to power, the Inter-American Press Association (IAPA) had charged that Communist Party cadres in Chile were threatening newspaper editors and menacing the freedom of the press. This charge came just a few days after Henry Kissinger at an off-the-record White House regional press briefing in Chicago offered the self-fulfilling prophecy that if the Chilean Congress confirmed Allende as president, the neighboring countries of Peru, Bolivia and Argentina would be threatened with the spread of communism. The IAPA is an organization of publishers of newspapers in North and South America, and it is dominated by powerful newspapers which reflect big-business interests. Augustín Edwards, publisher of *El Mercurio* of Santiago, is a former president of IAPA and a continuing influential member. IAPA returned to the charge at its meeting in Rio de Janeiro in May 1971, citing the action to make *El Mercurio* pay its delinquent taxes and the purchase of Zig-Zag as evidence that Allende was destroying the opposition press.

The IAPA offensive was still in high gear in October, when its Freedom of the Press Committee met in Chicago with a major Brazilian publisher as its chairman. Ignoring the actual censorship in Brazil, it charged the Allende regime with systematic operations "to control independent newspapers by doing away with their power to criticize and by provoking their economic demise," and prophesying that "the Chilean press is going through its last days of freedom."[15] These were charges which not even the harshest critics of the regime attempted to make inside Chile. Only a short time earlier, Juan de Onis had reported from Santiago to *The New York Times* that "there appears to be more press freedom in practice in Chile at this time than in many other Latin American countries. . . . There is no sector of political opinion that is not able to make known its views."[16] In October, Joseph Novitski, probably the most hostile member of *The New York Times* team toward the UP program, corroborated the de Onis analysis. "In fact, newspapers, radio news programs and television news and commentary programs in Santiago show greater freedom in expressing a wide range of views than those of several other South American countries, including Brazil and Peru."[17] And early the following year, Renato Poblete testified that the UP programs "have been taking place without suppression of freedom, with no control of the press, with normal congressional activity." Poblete, a Jesuit sociologist, had worked actively to prevent an Allende victory both in 1964 and 1970, and he subsequently continued to identify with the Christian Democrats.[18] But the IAPA did not give up easily. At Costa Rica, in March 1972, it was still shrieking that Chile was curbing press freedom, just two months after the *Miami Herald* had told its readers that the press in Chile was continuing on its "free and partisan way."[19] It was not until Allende in October 1972 talked for two hours to a 10-man delegation of IAPA officials that the association decided there were more glaring press problems in other countries than in Chile. And evidence from other sources, some of them unsympathetic, confirms that the press was not curbed at any time. "Chile remains today an open pluralistic society," William Montalbano reported to the *Miami Herald* in April 1972. "The press is free and vigorous."[20] More than a year later, Marvine Howe reported in similar terms to *The New York Times:* "The press is one of the freest in the world, but it can be irresponsible. . . . The right-wing

114

radio stations are particularly virulent, openly insulting the president and calling for his overthrow."[21] To which *Le Monde* of Paris added, in an editorial on Allende's overthrow—which it called a "tragedy" and a "crime"—that democracy had not come to an end in Chile under the UP coalition nor had the media been controlled.[22]

The first IAPA charges of restrictions on the press in 1971 had been received with scorn bordering on hilarity by the UP supporters. The point was vigorously made that the association was honoring the military dictatorship of Brazil with its iron censorship of the press by meeting in Rio, yet using its resources to criticize, not Brazil, but a country where everyone said openly what he thought. President Allende issued a refutation of the charges, which he ended with a challenge to Augustín Edwards, who had installed himself in Miami, Florida, as a vice president of Pepsi Cola, telling him that those who sought the protection of the law should themselves observe the law. "It would be interesting if you would communicate to one of the most conspicuous leaders of your association, Mr. Augustín Edwards," Allende wrote the IAPA officials, "that he should come to Chile to accept responsibility for the financial manipulations of his bank, manipulations which have put the general manager in prison."[23]

Even if the impact of such charges was slight within Chile, they helped to condition world opinion, especially opinion in the United States. As President Allende was well aware, and as he continued to stress publicly at all times, the generous cooperation of the United States was of paramount importance for the success of the political experiment he was directing. He had turned the other cheek to President Nixon's snubs, and while he insisted that the United States would not be allowed to interfere in Chile or with Chile's decisions, he actively sought good relations and committed himself to work within the Inter-American System.[24]

The press of the United States must bear a major part of the blame for the continued lack of response to Allende's overtures. While it is normally difficult to go beyond hunches and informed guesses in an evaluation of the influence of the press on a given event, the record in this instance is unusually clear. Since the beginning of 1971, a young Latin American specialist (Fred Goff) has been providing from an office in Berkeley, California, photocopies of all reports on Latin America published by the *Christian Science Monitor*, the *Wall Stree Journal*, the *New York Times*, the *Washington Post*, the *Miami Herald*, and the *Los Angeles Times*. It also provides the same news as reported in the *Guardian*, London (formerly the *Manchester Guardian*); and the weekly edition in English of *Le Monde* of Paris.[25] John C. Pollock, a member of the Chile Research Group at Rutgers University, New Jersey, has headed a team of sociologists which has made analyses of the clippings dealing with Chile and brought extraordinary assumptions and attitudes to light.

Pollock and his associates criticize the United States press for failing to put the events in Chile either in a historical context or in a comparative context. The Allende victory emerges simply as a happening, not as the culmination of a long and harsh struggle by the workers for recognition. Allende is blamed for failing to solve overnight the problems with which many preceding governments had wrestled unsuccessfully and which no neighboring country has solved. Imbedded in the coverage, both from the correspondents of the newspapers and from the wires of Associated Press and United Press International are five themes.

1 Allende is isolated from the vast majority of Chileans in his actions and goals.

2 Almost all threats to political stability and continuity are leftist in origin.

3 The middle and upper classes are the chief repositories of political wisdom and virtue.

4 Resentment against the United States transnational corporations is essentially irrational (and their nationalization is bound to engender production difficulties as key technical personnel pull out).

5 Allende's political and economic problems are of "crisis" proportions, and his successes are rarely mentioned, if at all.

The reporting isolated Allende in a variety of ways. He is always identified as a Marxist and head of a Marxist regime, whereas the president of Brazil is not similarly identified each time as a military dictator or the president of the United States as a Wall Street lawyer. Allende once chided the *New York Times* for this practice. "I think I'm a pretty ignorant man," he said in an interview, "but not ignorant enough to maintain that there are marxist governments. I think there are socialist governments, liberal governments and conservative governments. I believe that marxism is a scientific method for interpreting history and not a recipe for government."[26] But the lesson went unlearned. To the end, the word *marxist* appeared unfailingly in the lead paragraph. Isolation was also stressed by attributing actions to him, such as the nationalization of the copper industry, which were joint actions of Congress and the administration. The notion was implicit that by some strange quirk this one individual was responsible for all the problems, so that his disappearance would restore normality. Never did it come across that he was part of an historical process. That he would finally overstep himself and be caught, for all his cleverness, was guaranteed by the metaphors. For C. L. Sulzberger of the *New York Times*, he was "a light-tripping fox," an "acrobat," an "adroit juggler." Besides, he was not to be taken too seriously, a "plump little doctor" (*Newsweek*), a "former county coroner" (*Miami Herald*).

117

An interesting element brought out by the analysis is a switch in tone and structure several times. The most important change was a reduction in the level of hostility in January 1971, following a crescendo of warning before the presidential election and while the confirmation of Allende was in doubt. This lower profile corresponded with a similar change in tactics on the part of the transnationals which then hoped to make some deal with Allende as they had done with previous fire-eating presidents. When conflict with the transnationals rose again in the fall of 1971 with the announcement that excess profits cancelled out the claims to indemnification of the major copper companies, so did the tone of the press. Shifts in reporting thus correlated with related shifts in United States corporate fortunes and policies, and the assumptions in the press reports "paralleled the goals or decisions of major United States multinational corporations." The reason suggested by the analysts is, however, not a "conspiracy," though the consequence for the United States public is not thereby significantly eased. What they see is "a culturally derived perception of common interests," so that "the press acts not as a watchdog of big government and big business, but rather as their agreeable colleague, functioning as a 'voluntary arm of established power.' "

Both before and after Allende's election, the United States press "exhibited a flagrant pandering to Cold War stereotypes," presenting differences between Chile and the United States "as a conflict between the forces of marxism and socialism, on the one hand, and democracy and capitalism on the other." While Washington is criticized at times for presidential anger and diplomatic hostility, in part because such actions may be self-defeating, the assumption that United States intervention is justified on behalf of United States interests—understood as the interests of the transnational corporations—is almost universal. Typical was an article in the *New York Times* in October

118

1971 by Murray Rossant, president of the Twentieth Century Fund, presenting economic strangulation as an acceptable policy. The Allende government could be paralyzed, he wrote, by congressional sanctions, withholding of aid, exertion of maximum leverage on international lending agencies, pressure on banks and corporations, and manipulation of world copper prices.

Self-fulfilling prophecies of doom are also common. In a report prepared in October 1972, John and Michele Pollock had this comment. "Growing logically out of a reporting posture that emphasizes the leftist internal threat, the disaffection of the upper and middle sectors, and Allende's isolation and irrationality, is a view of Chilean politics as essentially catyclismic. Reports about both political and economic issues stop just short of suggesting that the upheaval they predict for Chile will be millenial in scope."

Perhaps the most dismal of all the failures of the United States press was the reporting of the March of the Empty Pots, December 1971, when some 5000 women demonstrated in Santiago against the food shortages. No attempt was made to place this women's demonstration in the historical perspective of the Family March with God for Liberty in São Paulo, Brazil, in March 1964, when right-wing movements helped prepare the emotional climate for the coming military seizure of power by a mass demonstration of women reciting the rosary to implore God to save Brazil from the "Bolshevist peril." Nor did the United States press give its readers any indication of the middle- and upper-class status of the marchers, this in sharp contrast to its stress on the class character of the crowds who two weeks earlier had welcomed Fidel Castro. Several accounts failed to mention that the march was spearheaded by 30 youths wearing hard helmets and carrying wooden clubs and rocks, this in contrast with the stress on "hard-hatted brigades of leftists" when the other side demonstrated. A *New York Times* editorial represented

119

the women as engaged in "a peaceful protest" and doing nothing more seditious than making "an unholy racket by banging their pots and pans and shouting anti-government slogans." In fact, as *Le Monde* of Paris and *Excelsior* of Mexico City correctly reported, this was a right-wing riot which the police were forced to break up when the president of Chile and his palace were stoned.

The perspective that was available to but ignored by the United States press was presented by *Latin America*, a weekly newsletter published in London. "No one denies that there are food shortages, although it is difficult to imagine women being better fed than those who marched the streets last week. In fact, all that they were complaining about was a decreased beef supply—hardly starvation." To justify this value judgment, the facts about the food shortages were immediately presented. Four pertinent points were noted. First, agricultural production had actually increased since Allende took office, thanks to the increased pace of agrarian reform. Second, this increase was less than it would otherwise have been, because big landowners had slaughtered reproductive cattle and failed to plant crops. Thirdly, there was a worldwide beef shortage which was not going to be corrected for at least ten years. Finally, in Chile there was an increased effective demand for food. "As a result of wage increases to lower paid workers when it took office over a year ago, the government is having to provide food for people who never ate either adequately or regularly previously. And as prices have been controlled by the government, their wage increases have not lost their initial impact."[28]

The impact of the media in Chile and in the United States on the ability of the Allende government to pursue its policies would become more evident later. At the end of its first year in office, however, things looked better than could have been anticipated. The gross national product, which had shown little progress in the previous years, was up an amazing eight percent in 1971. Unemployment was down to half the level of the previous year. The rate of increase in the cost of living, which had grown steadily for several years to 36 percent in 1970, was down to 23 percent. Real wages had increased 30 percent, and the price of food and other basic commodities had been kept low, while the new distribution system made supplies available everywhere. And all this had been done within the constitutional framework and without a single political prisoner anywhere in Chile. When Allende boasted that there were no political prisoners, his most virulent opponents did not dare challenge the claim.[29] But the war had only begun, the war of nerves with the Congress and other forces controlled by the opposition at home, and the invisible blockade abroad. The second year would give a better indication of the relative strength of the two sides.

5.

The Counterattack

Political instability was built into the Chilean situation in 1970 when the elections gave the executive branch to a coalition committed to major social change while leaving the legislature under the control of the elements who would be adversely affected by that change. Specific problems did not take long to surface. In January 1971, Congress rejected an administration request for a 15 percent surtax on corporate income taxes to finance higher government salaries. It was an issue clearly illustrating the political philosophy of the two sides. The Administration started from the principle that a few had an excessive share of the country's wealth and that it was essential to alter this situation. The other side simply wanted to maintain the existing inequality.

From that time onward, Congress consistently refused to appropriate funds for the administration's program of adjusting wages so as to achieve a more balanced distribution of the national income, chopping off a third of the budget submitted to it. The refusal to finance government programs left the administration with no choice but to print money, an inherently inflationary process. Price controls and increased production kept the inflation rate in 1971 far below the level of previous years, but the spiral was renewed by 1972.

The plan of economic disruption developed by the oligarchs included the diversion of food and other basic supplies into the black market. To curb this required laws to punish speculators and black-market operators, but Congress blocked all administration proposals, thus giving its protection to the anti-social activities.

The Chilean constitution requires a two-thirds majority of the Senate to remove a president by impeachment, but other officials can be removed by a simple majority of the Congress. This provision was used many times during the Allende term of office to disrupt government by impeaching cabinet ministers on politically motivated and highly questionable charges. In this way it forced out of office three ministers of the interior, the minister charged with domestic security and control of the police, two labor ministers, two economics ministers, a justice minister, and a minister of mines.

Congress in 1972 issued a direct challenge to the foundation stone of the UP program. It passed a constitutional amendment which would prohibit the administration from expropriating any kind of private property without specific legislation, backdating the prohibition to the introduction of the measure in October 1971. This would force the return of any industries taken after that date, including banks and others acquired by purchase of their stock or shares in the open market. The measure had been initiated by the Christian Democrats who took the position that the UP coalition was transferring too much of the economy to the "social sector." Congress, they claimed, should rule on each instance. When Allende exercised a veto, the Congress passed the measure again with a simple majority, claiming that a constitutional ambiguity gave it this power. A Constitutional Court had been created during the Frei regime, and all five members were Frei nominees. This tribunal had ruled on five constitutional issues since Allende came to power, supporting the position of the administration on all occasions. Allende sought to bring the new conflict to the same court, but Congress objected, claiming that the court lacked jurisdiction when the prerogatives of Congress were at issue. The matter remained unresolved. From that time, it continued to sour relations between Congress and the administration, and it enabled Allende's opponents to charge that he was acting unconstitutionally when he followed his interpretation of the constitution.

The conflict reached such proportions that the Congress, headed by Eduardo Frei as president of the Senate, established itself as a kind of anti-government. As early as March 1971, David F. Belnap of the Los Angeles Times, no friend of Allende, described Frei as "a behind-the-scenes compromiser," with "an elder-statesman 'complex,' " and with the ambition to lead a united opposition. This ambition he later fulfilled when the Christian Democrats linked themselves formally in opposition with the National Party, and he subsequently conducted himself as though he were the constitutional president of Chile, presenting the administration with one ultimatum after another. This finally built up to the point where the Christian Democrats called for a complete halt of the government's program, warning that if it failed to obey immediately, "the historic responsibility of what will happen in Chile will fall on its shoulders alone."[1]

The courts similarly took the side of the oligarchy at critical moments. The Supreme Court revealed its allegiances in January 1971 when by an eleven to two vote it reversed a decision of a military court, confirmed by the court of appeals, and refused to lift the parliamentary immunity of a senator who had been implicated in the plot in which General Schneider was killed. That same plot

produced yet another obvious example of "class justice."
General Roberto Viaux, who in 1968 had led a mini-revolt
of the army garrison in Tacna, was tried and found guilty
of planning the Schneider kidnap-killing operation, an
operation planned to create a state of political chaos which
would have prevented Allende from taking office. The
20-year sentence imposed on Viaux was reduced by a
higher court to two years (to be followed by five years'
exile), a prison term less than that regularly given to a
peasant found guilty of stealing chickens. Such weighting
of the scales of justice was constant. When Moises Huente-
laf, a peasant leader, was killed by a landowner during a
land takeover in the south of Chile, the landowner was
allowed to go free, but the 21 peasants involved in the
takeover were kept in jail for six months. On another
occasion, landowners whose land had already been expropriated came back to their former holdings one morning
and attempted to seize the machinery which was now the
property of the peasants. When unarmed peasants tried to
stop them, the former landowners shot and killed four.
The murderers were allowed to go free, and no charges
were ever pressed.[2]

The identification by the courts with the policies and
attitudes of the opposition prevented the government from
using the existing laws to curb abuses by the newspapers.
As generally in Latin America, strong laws existed in Chile
to protect the administration from the attacks of a highly
politicized press, and previous regimes had not hesitated to
use them. When the newspapers and radio stations controlled by the National Party and the Christian Democrats
escalated the normal political sniping to a campaign of
defamation of the president and his principal associates
calculated to incite the public to support a violent
overthrow of the regime, the administration invoked
these laws some 50 times but lost nearly every case. Even
when the facts were too obvious to permit an acquittal,

the penalties imposed were minimal. When the National Party ran an advertisement in *El Mercurio* calling on Chileans to reject the government as "illegitimate" and "unconstitutional," and to disobey all measures the government might propose, thus making an open incitement to insurrection, the government filed suit to have the paper closed for six days, but the courts reopened it after just one day. Meanwhile, the incident was used in the world press to trumpet the determination of the "Marxist" regime to destroy freedom of the press. The heading in the *New York Times* announced: "Court in Chile Shuts Paper Over Anti-Allende Ad." That headline carried two inferences, both false, that the closing was permanent or at least indefinite, and that this or any newspaper which carried advertising opposed to the regime—no matter how reasonable—could expect to be suppressed.

The office of the Comptroller General was similarly used to harass the administration and thwart its initiatives. Hector Humeres, the Comptroller, had been appointed to his office for twelve years by the Frei administration and was removable only by impeachment. When Allende took office, he set out to amplify his own powers—secure in the knowledge that an administration which lacked a majority in Congress could not touch him—pronouncing on the legality of projects as though he were the supreme court. Each time the administration brought an industry into the "social area," he ruled that the action was illegal, a ruling which froze all funds for that industry and brought production to a halt. Under the constitution, the president had to issue an "insistence decree" signed by all his cabinet ministers in order to override a ruling of the Comptroller. This worked for a time, but the opposition finally found a further ploy. The National Party introduced a measure in Congress to impeach all the ministers. Without a two-thirds majority, they could not touch the president, but a simple majority sufficed to impeach ministers.[3]

Trade and business associations of employers joined in a campaign orchestrated by the Confederation of Production and Commerce to bring about the economic chaos that would ensure military intervention. A verbal ambiguity proved extraordinarily helpful in this campaign. *Gremio*, a generic word in Spanish for any kind of voluntary association, from a church guild to the governing body of a university, is commonly used in Chile to designate either an association of employers or a trade union. The press both in Chile and the United States took advantage of this ambiguity to create the impression that work stoppages which were in fact lock-outs engineered by *gremios* of employers were strikes of workers protesting the policies of the UP government.

The top people in the oligarchy were involved in the organization of this campaign. The Confederation of Production and Commerce is an umbrella organization for the five largest associations of the owners of the means of production and distribution in the country. These are the Association of Manufacturers (SOFOFA), the National Society of Agriculture (SNA), the Chamber of Commerce, and the Chilean Construction Chamber. The fifth pillar of the Confederation was the National Mining Society, the power of which was undercut by the nationalization of the big mines.

A major part of the Confederation's strategy was to enlist on its side a number of *gremios* consisting mainly of members of the middle sectors or privileged workers. Of these, the key group was the trucking industry. In a country more than 2,500 miles from end to end and with few railroads, the most powerful industry is trucking, without which food distribution is impossible. The industry has long been organized on the basis of owner-operators of a single truck. The truck represented for its owner his entire capital, and since insurance was prohibitively expensive, he entrusted the truck to nobody but

127

himself. Many of the trucks were old and patched, dependent for survival on a constant flow of parts from the United States. These truckers were tough, self-reliant men, the modern version of the *gaucho* who earlier gave its flavor to the countryside in Chile as in Argentina. More recently, a new element had come into trucking. Many big landowners developed fleets of trucks, using the money they received from the land reform during the Frei administration. They bought diesel-powered trucks from Europe and operated them with paid drivers on normal commercial lines. They were little affected by the choking off by the United States of spare parts for the old gasoline-powered vehicles of the independents. Their newer vehicles needed fewer parts, and besides the channels to Europe always remained open for those who could afford to buy.

The independent truckers were consequently the first powerful group to suffer significantly as a result of the "invisible blockage" imposed on Chile, and their sense of outrage was not eased when they saw the modern diesel-powered trucks continuing to function normally while they were immobilized or had to pay exorbitant black-market prices for what they needed to keep moving. The right-wing leaders played on this dissatisfaction, assuring the independents that they could count on total support by the big truck companies, which controlled some 25 percent of the entire trucking industry, in any action they might take to challenge the regime. They even undertook to pay truckers for not transporting goods, and reportedly used dollars supplied by United States interests for this purpose.[4]

Other gremios sympathetic to the plots of the Federation included such upper-middle-class groups as doctors and lawyers, the latter in particular always conservative in Chile, and such middle-class elements as small shopkeepers. As political scientist James Petras has noted, "from the beginning of the century, whenever the middle-class parties faced a mass, independent working-class movement, they took the side of the traditional Right, set aside disagreements, and watched hundred and thousands of workers jailed or murdered. . . . The Chilean middle class, either because it lacked property or because its property was insignificant, depended on and was subordinate to large landowning groups and large foreign concerns."[5]

While individuals, like some of the truckers, might be squeezed by such things as a lack of spares for their trucks, the people who formed the constituency of the opposition were not revolting against a state of misery, as were those who looked to Allende for salvation. The real contrast is well brought out in a report prepared for the Committee for Peace and Justice of the Association of Chicago Priests by a group of priest sociologists, some of whom lived in Chile in 1972 and 1973. "It is important," they say, "to realize how well middle classes (a *minority* of the population) were living in Chile. The most ordinary middle-class family could count on having at least one maid, usually a Mapuche Indian girl paid next to nothing and often treated half like a pet, half like a beast of burden. Lunch and supper in middle-class homes meant four to six-course meals, and meat meant only steak. The first banging of pots and pans was to protest the lack of steak. Until January of this year (1973), meat other than beef was quite available. The Right [i.e., the upper class] and the upper-middle class remained comfortable through all the hardships, for whatever they need was at their fingertips on the black market—only a phone call away. The lower-middle and the poor could not afford to buy there, so supply exceeded demand, although prices were as much as ten times as high as official prices. The government tried to fight the black market, but it could not do so without laws, which the legislature refused to pass."[6]

Within organized labor itself, there was also an important division which the Federation was quick to exploit.

As in other Latin American countries, the *empleados* and the *obreros*—a distinction approximately equal to white-collar and blue-collar workers—have separate gremios and other status symbols to mark their sense of belonging to different classes. Each group in the same enterprise has its contract, different scales of benefits and legal minimum wages. Even the political affiliation of the respective unions was frequently different, the *obreros* being close to the Socialist and Communist parties, while the *empleados* looked to the Christian Democrats or the Communists. The Right did succeed in getting some gremios of *empleados* to strike, and the opposition press in Chile, as also the press of the United States, trumpeted such actions as a demonstration that the workers were turning against Allende. The issue would become critical in 1973. It will be pursued later.

The pressures against the Allende regime inside Chile were fully orchestrated with the outside pressures exercised by the government and business interests of the United States. Here Chile's major weakness was the enormous debt inherited by Allende, coupled with the structural distortions—also inherited—which forced Chile to import vast amounts of food to survive. While food production had already begun to grow in 1971 as a result of the land reform, it would take several years to catch up with the increased consumption caused by redistribution of income in favor of the previously hungry masses.

The inherited foreign debt totalled more than $3 billion, much of it held by United States interests. Chile had for many years financed a deficit in its balance of trade by foreign borrowings. During the seven years preceding the nationalization of copper in 1971, it obtained more than $1 billion from the World Bank, the Inter-American Development Bank, the Eximbank and US-AID. Reserves at the end of 1970 amounted to about $350 million, and lines of credit totalling $219 million were available to facilitate normal trading. At the beginning of 1971, the Eximbank gave $27 million and the Inter-American Development Bank, $11 million. But these were the only new loans subsequent to Allende's election. All other United States sources dried up, except for some AID loans for military aid and a small AID program that did not help the balance of payments. The lines of credit quickly shrunk to $32 million. In addition, the drop in copper prices cut Chile's anticipated income, the loss being estimated at $187 million in two years. As against this, there were some credits from socialist countries, the principal one being $300 million from the Soviet Union. Most of this, however, was tied to the import of heavy industrial goods. While it would provide long-term benefits, it did not ease the immediate need of spare parts and supplies for an economy totally integrated into the United States system. Chile had to live on its dwindling reserve of foreign exchange, which in two years was down to $80 million.[7]

Seeking to anticipate and avoid a crisis, Chile announced in November 1971 that it wanted to renegotiate debts totalling more than $3 billion, a process that had become routine for poor countries saddled with heavy debts and faced with unanticipated complications, such as the fall in copper prices and the resultant deterioration of the terms of trade. In an extremely detailed and conciliatory statement, President Allende insisted that Chile would honor all its commitments to the limit of its possibilities. He said that repayments of $300 million were due in 1971, $400 million in 1972, and a further $400 million in 1973, most of it to the United States. He undertook to continue payments on schedule to the World Bank and the Inter-American Development Bank, as well as some short-term debts, but announced a moratorium on other repayments while renegotiation terms were worked out.[8]

The United States responded with a war of nerves. Unidentified Washington spokesmen let it be known through the press that they were extremely sympathetic but that the European members of the Paris Club took a very negative view of any country that didn't pay its debts as they became due. The Paris Club is an informal association of sixteen industrial nations which coordinates their monetary policies toward poor countries. But before the Club could meet, the United States took several steps to damage Chile's prestige and creditworthiness. Of these, the most outrageous was a statement to the press from Herbert G. Klein, White House Director of Communications, and Robert H. Finch, Counselor to the President. Returning from a quick "fact-finding" trip in Latin America (which did not include Chile), they told the press that the "feeling" among Latin Americans was that Allende "won't last long."[9] Next came an announcement that Chile was $20 million in arrears to the Eximbank, and that the United States had refused a requested 90-day extension, and would suspend credit guarantees and insurance to Chile "until there is further clarification of Chile's unilateral moratorium on debt payment."[10]

When the Club met, it quickly became apparent that the European members, especially France and Spain, were highly sympathetic to Chile, and that the opposition was being organized and led by the United States which wanted no discussion of rescheduling loans until Chile first agreed to pay the copper companies the full amount they were demanding as compensation. One ploy was the offer of an International Monetary Fund (IMF) loan on terms which would subject Chile's internal economic decisions to IMF control, thus limiting its political options. The United States argued strongly in support of this proposal, while arguing equally strongly against the application of the same terms to a proposed loan to Argentina, whose military dictatorship was being courted by Washington. Chile rejected the proposal as offensive to its dignity and a violation of its sovereignty.[11] After two months of stalling, the United States said it would not insist on the IMF conditions if Chile gave "acceptable assurances" of payment to United States firms taken over. Under pressure from the Europeans, the United States finally accepted a compromise formula which left everything still in the air, a Chilean promise of "just compensation for all nationalizations in conformity with Chilean and international law."[12]

The immediate reason for the acceptance by the United States of this compromise was loss of face and prestige as a result of the revelation by Washington columnist Jack Anderson of the ITT memoranda describing the conspiracy to block Allende's election and to create economic chaos in Chile when he was elected. The extent of the Washington Administration's involvement would not emerge until a subsequent congressional investigation, and spokesmen for the administration tried at first to question the authenticity of the documents and downgrade their importance. But the circumstantial evidence was excessive. Too many of the things which the conspirators had urged had in fact followed. In Chile, 80,000 copies of a book containing the original documents with a Spanish translation were sold out as quick as they came off the presses. All around the world, the revelations made headline news. The result was a big boost both at home and abroad for the Allende regime. A movement rapidly developed in Chile to confiscate without indemnification all ITT property in the country on the ground that the company had engaged in a treasonable conspiracy against Chile, a proposal which Allende after some hesitation accepted. ITT had six affiliates in Chile, with 7,900 employees, of whom 6,000 were in the telephone company. It valued the telephone company alone at $153 million. The company had already been "intervened" in September 1971, when four officials were charged with fraud.

Any international sympathy ITT might have enjoyed was dissipated as it became known that it had been engaging in a huge double cross. While assuring other United States companies with assets in Chile, including the copper companies, that it would maintain a common front, it secretly urged the Chileans to give it better terms, saying that the copper take-over was protected by the constitutional amendment, but failure to pay ITT would create a very negative world image. This technique had worked in Peru in 1969 when ITT received compensation for nationalized holdings, while a Standard Oil subsidiary did not. Chile in fact offered to submit to experts of the International Telecommunications Union, a UN entity, the task of assessing for compensation the value of the telephone company, but this did not satisfy ITT. It was covered by insurance with a United States government agency to the extent of $109 million against expropriation, and it presumably believed this was more than an independent arbitrator would give it. Chile valued the property at $25 million and said ITT had maintained an inflated book value so that it could repatriate more of its profits. Such repatriation was fixed by law at ten percent of book value each year. Chile would also have raised in arbitration the issue of the quality of ITT's equipment and service, which it claimed had not kept in step with world developments. In 1940, Chile had 1.77 phones per 100 inhabitants, which was 93 percent of the world average. In 1970, with 3.12 phones per 100 inhabitants, it was down to 51 percent of the world average. And the proportion of calls not completed was eight times the world average.[13]

In addition to resolving the IMF issue in Chile's favor after the ITT exposures, the Paris Club in mid-1972 reached satisfactory agreement on broad principles of renegotiation, leaving details to be worked out bilaterally. Chile quickly resolved the details with all countries involved except the United States. Washington continued to drag its feet while United States companies stepped up their economic offensive against Chile. Kennecott in September asked a French court to block payment to Chile for copper sold in France on the ground that it still held a 49 percent interest. French dockers, sympathetic to Chile, refused to unload the ship. It was diverted to Holland, became embroiled in new legal actions, then returned to France, where courts began a long battle which left unsettled for an indefinite period the ownership of the copper. Similar actions were started in Sweden, Germany and Italy, causing potential buyers to look for copper from other sources and damaging Chile's credit standing. European banks suspended negotiations of $200 million in lines of credit and Dutch and Canadian lines of credit were cut because of increased risk.

Chilean government officials reported that many other United States transnationals followed a similar strategy, though more subtly. They insisted on cash in advance rather than the normal 30 to 120 days grace, higher payments, special forms of payment, the purchase of unwanted products along with those sought. Some said they were involved in negotiations in which it was obvious that the other party was not just seeking protection against risk but determined to prevent a sale under any conditions. Thus, Sergio Bitar, Chile's minister of mines, said the Chilean Copper Company had agreed to buy heavy multimillion dollar trucks from an Australian company, but the Australians reneged when Kennecott said it would never buy from the company again.[14]

The Chileans made another effort in mid-December 1972 to reach a solution of the financial conflict with the United States. They may have hoped, when they asked for the meeting, that they would arrive with a guarantee from Leonid Brezhnev that he would take care of them if the United States refused. Instead, what Allende had just learned in Moscow was that Nixon had got there before him and included in his deal a commitment from Brezhnev to stay on the sidelines. In consequence, no progress was registered at the Washington meeting. Three months later, the Chileans tried again. As soon as it became clear at the new meeting that the unresolved issue was always the same, namely, the United States refusal to accept the legitimacy of the formula established by the Chilean Congress to determine compensation, Chile's negotiators invoked a treaty into which the United States and Chile had entered in 1916. Its purpose was to resolve conflicts for which normal diplomatic channels had failed.

The treaty established a permanent 5-member international commission, each country naming one national and one non-national, and the two countries agreeing on a chairman. The membership had most recently been renewed during the presidency of John F. Kennedy. Madam Suzan Bastid, professor of international law at the University of Paris, was chairman. Chile's nominees were Edmundo Vargas, professor of international law at the University of Chile, and Manfred Lachs, Polish international law expert and judge at the International Court of the Hague. Both United States nominees had died and not been replaced.

The United States negotiators did not challenge the existence or validity of the treaty but made it clear that they were not going to follow that route. The treaty involves a long series of processes. The commission has a year to prepare a report on any question submitted to it, after which each country has six months to study the report and try to reach agreement. If this fails, the question goes to the International Court of the Hague, with certain exceptions. But once the United States agreed to this process, it could no longer argue that Chile was defaulting on its obligations, and that was the line it sought to maintain and to impose by whatever sanctions it chose. But for Chile the rule of law was paramount, as ultimately the only protection of the weak against the strong. Accordingly, when Allende went to Buenos Aires in May

1973 to attend the inauguration of the Argentine president, he sought a meeting with Secretary of State William Rogers, at which Rogers promised a formal statement from Washington regarding the application of the treaty provisions within three weeks. That statement was never issued. By that time, Washington had presumably reached the conclusion that the policy of keeping Chile dangling and in permanent crisis was not only working but would soon bring decisive results, as in fact it did.[15]

The permanent crisis may be said to date from September 1972. Six months earlier, rightist extremists developed an action program to put into effect the long-projected objective of economic chaos, with September as the target date for action under the name of "Plan Septiembre." The date was delayed until October when in September the government removed a high army officer, General Canales. A start was, however, made by the creation of two vigilante groups in wealthy areas of Santiago, *Protección Comunal* (joint protection), and *Soberanía, Orden y Libertad* (sovereignty, order and liberty).

October witnessed a situation without historic precedent, a withholding of the means of production by the owners, combined with a lock-out by employers. The key element was the gremio of the truck owners. The previous month the truckers had struck for higher tariffs and the government had quickly agreed to the reasonableness of their case and approved a major increase. But trucking was one of the industries scheduled for nationalization as an essential utility, and in October León Vilarín, a Christian Democrat and national head of the truckers' organization, ordered a new stoppage without consulting most of the unions. When the government moved to end the stoppage on the ground that urgently needed supplies were not moving, the Christian Democrats protested that the legitimate right of workers to strike was being challenged. With them in support of the work stoppage were all the reactionary elements in Chile, the national organization of big farmers (SNA) and of big industrialists (SOFOFA), the national organization of distributors of merchandize, the associations of doctors, lawyers and engineers, the conservative National Party, and the fascist Fatherland and Freedom organization.[16]

Before the October work stoppage, the independent truckers had been little politicized. They were typical small businessmen, each concerned with keeping his single truck, his entire livelihood, on the road. But the stoppage imposed from above opened the eyes of many. Goons moved in to sabotage the trucks of those who tried to carry on. Soon, various regional organizations of truckers realized that they were being used for political maneuvers of the Christian Democrats and told their members to get back to work. The impact of the operation did not, however, end there. The exposure by the Right of the power it had to destroy the country produced an extraordinary response from the working-class communities which surround Santiago. These fall into two categories. The older and more prosperous are the *cordones industriales*, the heavy concentrations (literally, banks or belts) of industry, with the living quarters of the workers adjacent. The others are the slums which have mushroomed in the last 20 years wherever the constant flow of migrants from the countryside could establish a foothold. Many of these slums have been well organized, and especially since 1970, the government had provided materials to enable the dwellers to put up decent homes, creating neighborhoods known as *campamentos*. Employment for those who live there is still precarious, many involved in meaningless or unproductive service occupations, but a considerable number also have been given jobs in construction and other public services since 1970. While the Christian Democrats had cultivated these groups with some success, the process of politicization had been conducted principally by the

138

Communist Party, the Socialist Party, and especially MIR. From its modest beginnings as a student movement seven years earlier at the University of Concepcion, MIR had grown in numbers and stature and was now widely recognized as the leading edge of the Chilean revolution. Its subsidiaries covered the groups previously most neglected, the Revolutionary Peasant Movement among Indians and migrant farm workers, the Front of Revolutionary Workers in the factories, and the Movement of Revolutionary Slum Dwellers in the *callampas* and *campamentos*. In addition it has the University Movement of the Left for college students, and the Front of Revolutionary Students for high school youngsters twelve years and up. Before the 1970 election, one of its leaders, Victor Toro, said it was stockpiling arms and Molotov cocktails and training its members for combat. After the election, it announced it was keeping its arms but it reduced the previous level of illegal activities, engaging mostly in seizure of rural and urban land. Its top leaders were Miguel and Edgardo Enriquez, sons of the president of the University of Concepción. Another important leader was Andrés Pascal Allende, nephew of the president.

MIR played a principal part in the organization of the response to the October lock-outs. In each *cordón* or industrial sector, a committee representing the workers of all the factories was formed. It ordered the seizure of any factory closed by its owners, named a new management team, and resumed production and distribution. Simultaneously, it established organizations to mobilize and train the members of the community in maintaining order and defending the factories from any outside force. In the housing areas, as well as in the *campamentos* of the slum dwellers, the residents were organized into *comandos comunales* (community commands) which incorporated such previously existing units as industrial unions, health boards, neighborhood committees, centers for mothers,

139

student groups, and (in semi-rural areas) farm workers. The *comando* assumed responsibility for distribution of food and other supplies, political education, and the creation of self-defense forces. The philosophy behind this rapid and extraordinary development was quite clearly that of MIR, namely, that Chile was divided into those who had power and would use it to maintain privilege, and those who would always be underdogs until they built their own counterpower. While the committees and the commandos supported the UP government, they maintained their distance from it, moving to ever more radical stands as polarization intensified.[17] This mobilization of the workers proved a key element in the defeat of the right-wing efforts to strangle the government without having to resort to the use of armed forces. For example, when the employers offered two months' vacation with pay to their workers as a mid-summer (our winter) break later in 1972, the workers refused to take more than their regular three weeks. The workers had become the defenders of productivity against their own employers.

The opening of the rightist offensive produced strains within the UP coalition also. In spite of the many ideological strands it incorporated, it had held together remarkably for two years. The pressures from the more extreme elements both within the coalition and supporting it from farther left grew significantly, and President Allende recognized their reasonableness. "If obstacles are artificially created," he said in an interview, "if there is a conspiracy of ultrareactionary sectors, if the current attempt to provoke economic chaos is accentuated, we'll be forced to take our steps more quickly and decisively, that is, the process could be radicalized, because we have no choice." At the same time, he was as determined as ever to stay within the law and the constitution, and this led him to attempt two initiatives which some of his own coalition thought useless or dangerous. He appealed to the Christian

140

Democrats, who in July had joined with the National Party in a formal coalition called the United Democratic Federation (FDU), to engage in talks designed to establish an area of common interest in which the government could count on support. This effort to reach an understanding with the Christian Democrats was renewed several times, always on the basis that a loyal opposition was essential to prevent the destruction of the country's political institutions, but there was never a response. The other initiative did have significant short-term results. Allende brought three leaders of the armed forces into the cabinet, including General Carlos Prats, the universally respected commander-in-chief whose commitment to constitutional processes was known to parallel that of Allende himself. Prats was placed in charge of public order as minister of the interior.

The value of the move became evident in January 1973 when the opposition mounted a violent resistance to the government's proposals to move "massively and drastically" against the black market. That this move would include some system of rationing was clear from a government study which showed that the total food supply—including imports—had grown by 27 percent in two years, twice as much as in the previous five, but that consumption had grown even faster. The situation had been complicated by inadequate transportation and warehousing facilities, as well as a black market which had canceled out many of the effects of the income distribution and halved the quantity of goods available for the official network of distribution.

Counting on the enormous emotional resistance to rationing, *El Mercurio* charged that the country was in the "shadow of dictatorship." But Allende defused the opposition campaign, based on the slogan that the plan meant "political control via the stomach," by instituting only a form of rationing at the wholesale level, a state monopoly of distribution and sale of agricultural products, and put-

141

ting the armed forces in charge of the operation. The Right knew it could not accuse the armed forces of favoritism. The boycott announced by the gremios of farmers and industrialists, a boycott in which the central chamber of commerce urged its shopkeeper members to join, was quickly abandoned.[18]

The official stand of the Catholic church led by Cardinal Silva of Santiago continued at this time to favor Allende in his efforts to maintain the constitutional evolution by reducing polarization. Speaking to the delegates who had come to Chile for the meeting of UN Trade and Development group (UNCTAD) the previous March, Cardinal Silva had said that "Christians often ignore the drama of our human underdevelopment and overcrowding—unhealthy, promiscuous, dulling the moral sense of the people," an obvious endorsement of the social changes being introduced. Shortly afterward, at their annual meeting, the Chilean bishops expressed approval of the progress toward justice and equality being made by the present government, while warning that violence and propaganda were "poisoning the nation," this at a moment when the Right was intensifying its propaganda and developing its plans for violence. Again in January 1973, at the height of the conflict over rationing, the church authorities said it was proper that every home in the country should have its fair share of the basic foodstuffs available.[19]

The Cardinal's own influence was, however, being affected by the polarization which reached all levels of the church as of the country. At one end were the Christians for Socialism who in April 1972 had organized an Encounter with more than 400 delegates from Chile and all parts of Latin America which gave a clear option for socialism and affirmed the class war as an observable fact. At the other extreme, some priests and professing lay people supported the fascist Fatherland and Freedom group. The majority presented themselves as nonpolitical but inter-

142

preted this in practice as an identification with the position of the Christian Democrats and followed that party in its ever more total identification with the Right.

Probably more influential, however, than either Cardinal Silva or General Prats in keeping a majority of those who identified with the objectives of the Right from pursuing the policy of open violence which the extremists urged was the belief that the congressional elections in March 1973 would provide the United Democratic Federation with the two-thirds majority in the Senate it needed to impeach Allende. That would mean victory without open violation of the constitution. The belief seemed reasonable. Allende in 1970 had secured only 36 percent of the votes against a divided opposition. The rural bias in voting for Congress further favored the conservative wing, and the traditional trend of mid-term elections—as in the United States—was toward the opposition.

The campaign was extremely bitter, with Eduardo Frei acting as leading spokesman for the opposition and presenting the coming vote as a referendum. The UP coalition updated its program and promised radical innovations if given control of Congress. They would establish a one-chamber legislature and give the people the right to initiate legislation by a petition carrying 5,000 signatures. Replying in February to a new outbreak of right-wing violence, Allende warned the Right that if it continued obstruction and provocation, "the Chilean revolution would be forced to abandon the democratic road and embrace physical violence as an instrument." Neither the government nor the people wanted violence, he said, "but if counterrevolutionary violence is used against us, then we will use revolutionary violence." Allende also charged that the opposition was organizing another "strike of bosses," and the president of the confederation of small industry and traders answered that a national strike would indeed be called if the government did not change its economic policy. Mu-

143

tual accusations of terrorism became commonplace. One rightist candidate for senator, a retired colonel, praised Hitler and said a coup d'état could provide a solution for a country "in an emergency."

The elections were a striking success for the UP coalition without solving any of its problems. For the first time in Chile's history, the government improved its position in mid-term elections. Eighty percent of the 4.5 million registered voters went to the polls, the overall totals being 1,589,025 for UP and 2,003,047 for the opposition. This brought the UP percentage to 43.39 from the 36.2 of 1970. The elections renewed the entire 150-man Assembly and half the 50-man Senate. The government improved its position slightly in both houses but the opposition retained a majority in each, with 30 senators and 87 deputies, a loss of two and six respectively. The possibility of impeaching the president had evaporated.[20]

6.

Mobilization for Violence

In addition to the boost of the election results, the UP regime got another unexpected benefit in March 1973. Hearings of a Senate subcommittee on multinational corporations in Washington not only confirmed the charges made the previous year about ITT's efforts to prevent Allende becoming president and to create economic chaos after he was elected, but revealed that the Nixon Administration had taken a far more active and aggressive part in these activities than suggested by the earlier reports.

This news provided the setting for a meeting in April of 300 delegates from 60 countries in the World Assembly of Trade Unions. They met in Santiago as an expression of the support of workers everywhere for the workers of Chile in their efforts "to meet the affront of the Kennecott Company that has ordered the embargo of Chilean copper in various ports of the world." Addressing the delegates, President Allende charged that the big foreign corporations had even attempted to develop a counterrevolution. "The actions of the multinational corporations today constitute the most dangerous menace to the dignity of our peoples," he said. The Assembly concurred. In its final statement it characterized the multinationals as "instruments of the capitalistic monopolies of the United States, Western Europe and Japan, . . . threats against the sovereignty of nations, . . . instruments of pressure against the movement for social and political emancipation."[1]

Such evidences of increased support for the government merely drove the opposition to more desperate responses. Cheated by the elections of the hope of a two-thirds majority in the Senate to impeach the president, it intensified its offensive on all fronts. Economic sabotage was stepped up. Vital sectors of the economy were shut down. Charges against cabinet ministers were multiplied, and the orderly processes of government were interrupted more frequently than before by bringing impeachment charges against cabinet members, who could be ousted by a simple majority in Congress. The conflict with Congress entered a more acute stage when the president in April vetoed a bill which would have made the state-owned enterprises, rather than private industry, finance wage increases. Congress claimed that it could override the veto by a simple majority, and the Constitutional Tribunal ruled itself unqualified to resolve a dispute between Congress and the Executive.

The refusal of Congress to pass laws needed to curb black marketing prevented full implementation of the program to control food distribution. A report of the group known as United States Christians in Chile places the proportion controlled by the state at 30 percent. "A good deal of the part controlled by the private sector goes directly to the black market where prices are so high that the majority of the Chilean population cannot afford to buy through this channel. It is not uncommon, for example, to see upper-class Chilean women selling chickens from the trunks of their cars in the upper-class neighborhoods of Santiago for five and six times the official government price. With its still large profits, the opposition has invested in speculation rather than production. These speculators purchase everything from cigarettes to houses and sell them a few months later for two or three times their purchase price."[2]

A partial work stoppage at the El Teniente copper mine in June was the occasion of much misrepresentation in the press in Chile and in the United States. The miners were represented as turning from the government because it had failed to grant them a 41 percent wage increase approved by the legislature the previous year, and the administration was charged with violating the law by withholding part of the miners' wages. The facts were significantly different. The government had given all workers a 100 percent wage increase to compensate for increases in the cost of living. However, the miners had a clause in their contract entitling them to a 50 percent readjustment for inflation, and the opposition argued that they should get this increase in addition to the 100 percent granted all workers. The copper miners had long been a privileged group among workers, the high level of profits in the industry enabling the companies to pay them far more than other sectors of the economy could afford. When benefits were added to the cash salary, the average miner earned four times as much as other industrial workers. To give them yet another discriminatory wage increase would increase the differential further.

Various United States newspapers reported that 12,000 workers were on strike at El Teniente out of a total work force of 12,750, whereas at least 70 percent of the workers stayed on the job when the strike was called, and more than 90 percent of the *obreros* continued to work. The main support for the strike was among the *empleados*, largely controlled by Christian Democrat unions. Newspapers controlled by the Christian Democrats and by the National Party urged all workers in the country to participate in sympathy strikes, but with little success. To embarrass the government further, they impeached the minister for mines and the minister of labor on the ground that they were breaking the law by refusing to grant the additional increases. But the workers held firm against all enticements, and those who had struck returned to work on the terms originally laid down by the government.[3]

The American Institute for Free Labor Development (AIFLD) was active in the effort to detach a part of Chilean labor from its support of the UP regime and its objectives. Established in 1962 as part of the Alliance for Progress, this organization presented itself as seeking to upgrade Latin American trade unionism by incorporating the values and attitudes which made trade unionism strong in the United States. George Meany, president of AFL-CIO, is also president of AIFLD. J. Peter Grace, president of W.R. Grace, is its Board Chairman. Its role was described as follows by Grace: "Through the AIFLD, business, labor and government have come together to work toward a common goal in Latin America, namely, supporting the democratic form of government, the capitalist system, and general well-being of the individual. It is an outstanding example of a national consensus effectively at work for the national interest of the United States and for the best interests of the people of Latin America."

A basic tenet of AIFLD is that Latin American trade unionism tends to be "politically oriented" and that it must eliminate this element in order to grow and achieve economic power. But its practical application of this principle reveals a very curious understanding of what is and what is not political. Its executive director, William C. Doherty, boasted to a Senate committee that the graduates of its Institute at Port Royal, Virginia, had helped to plan and carry out the overthrow of a constitutional Latin American government. "As a matter of fact," he said "some of them were so active that they became intimately involved in some of the clandestine operations of the revolution before it took place on April 1. What happened in Brazil on April 1 (1964) did not just happen. It was planned, and planned months in advance. Many of the trade union leaders—some of whom were actually trained in our Institute—were involved in the revolution, and in the overthrow of the Goulart regime." Other AIFLD officials have boasted of their part in the overthrow of the Jagan government in Guyana in 1963.[4]

Board Chairman Peter Grace has also explained what being nonpolitical means. "AIFLD trains Latin Americans in techniques of combatting communist infiltration. This training has paid off handsomely in many situations. For instance, AIFLD trainees have driven communists from port unions which were harassing shipping in Latin America. After several years of effort, AIFLD men were able to take over control of the port union in Uruguay which had long been dominated by the communists. AIFLD men also helped drive communists from control in British Guiana. They prevented the communists from taking over powerful unions in Honduras and helped to drive the communists from strong 'jugular' unions in Brazil."[5]

In addition to training programs at Port Royal, AIFLD sends picked students to an advanced course in labor economics at George Washington University, and also holds seminars in Latin American countries. A report for the first ten years listed 79 Chileans as having studied at Port Royal, six at George Washington, and 8,837 at seminars in Chile. An AIFLD memorandum dated February 1973 says 108 Chileans, representing about a hundred professional unions and trade unions, had graduated from its training. They were concentrated in transportation and communications, sectors which led the work stoppages of October 1972 and July-August 1973. This represented a big jump in graduates in one year, reflecting the high priority given to this activity by the State Department, when practically all other AID programs had been stopped.

Since 1967, most of AIFLD's funds come from US-AID, this without any reduction in the business representation in its directorate.

As polarization intensified in Chile after the March 1973 elections, it became steadily clearer that the victory would ultimately lie—at least in the short term—with the side that could command the loyalty of the armed forces. Everyone knew there were tensions within the armed forces reflecting those in society. A recent sociological study had shown that most high-ranking officers were from upper-class or upper-middle-class families, most middle-ranking officers from the middle class, and most lower-ranking officers, recruits and conscripted soldiers and sailors from the peasantry and the industrial working class. The class identification, however, tended to have its own characteristics. A heavy weighting in the ranks in favor of rural recruits meant that many who joined up had little class consciousness or political awareness. Rather, they shared the peasant's traditional acceptance of National Party leadership, and the experience in the armed forces was not calculated to change this attitude. Career soldiers and sailors at all levels would tend to see themselves as the beneficiaries of upward social mobility and thus tend to be more conservative than their civilian peers.

Another important influence on attitudes of the Chilean armed forces was the orientation given them by their Pentagon mentors. Chile joined the other Latin American nations in 1947 in signing the Inter-American Mutual Defense Treaty, the purpose of which was to extend the "protection" of the United States to any signatory threatened by communist attacks. The United States defense planners began with the correct assumption that Latin American armies had not played and would not play a role in the world balance of power, and that their military importance would become progressively less with the growing sophistication of weaponry. But the Cold War would long divide the world along ideological lines, the "atheistic communism" of the Soviet Union challenging the "democratic Christianity" of the West. Latin American armed forces could protect their coasts against invasion, and also deal with internal subversion. The former objective was quickly eliminated when the development of long-range missiles changed the strategy of major war. The importance of the latter grew with the parallel success of Castro in Cuba and the expansion of Castro-inspired guerrillas in other countries.

A program of United States military aid to Chile began in 1952, and it was expanded in 1963 with a program for training and equipping anti-insurgency forces. From the outset, Washington recognized that the attitudes, mentality and assumptions of Chile's armed forces, as well as their battle-readiness, were critical to the safeguarding of the United States interests in the southern part of the hemisphere. It accordingly contributed between 1950 and 1970 more military aid to Chile—a total of $176 million—than to any other Latin American country except Brazil. This aid represented about a tenth of Chile's defense budget for the period. A further $2.4 million went to the Carabineros, the 26,000-man force of professional national police, between 1961 and 1970. Aid to police forces leans heavily on the teaching of interrogation methods of suspects which church-related and other independent investigative agencies have characterized as torture. Substantial funds have also been invested in bringing Chileans for training in the United States and in the Panama Canal Zone, and in sending United States military instructors and "advisers" to Chile. Nearly 4,000 Chileans were trained in the Panama Canal Zone since 1950, and the average number of United States military personnel in Chile, identified as such, has been 48 over the past decade. Of 201 Latin American military receiving special training in the Canal Zone in the late summer of 1973, 53 were from Chile.

151

The ideology behind the training was described by General William Westmoreland, chief of staff of the United States Army, at the Eighth Conference of the American Armies held in Rio de Janeiro in September 1968. Westmoreland had just completed four years as commander-in-chief in Vietnam. "One only needs to read one's newspaper," he said, "to know that the communists have used insurgent warfare throughout the world with varying degrees of success. . . . I feel that the prospect of repeated 'Vietnams' around the world presents a very real danger to the security of every freedom-loving people. For this reason I believe that the techniques of insurgent warfare are high on the list of threats which each of us must consider. As I said, we must not expect to find the patterns identical or the techniques always similar. Lenin built his revolution around the proletarian worker. Mao used the peasant as the backbone of his movement. In South Vietnam, Ho Chi Minh is relying on an insurgent trained outside the target country and on an army infiltrated from the same direction. Two things, however, are likely to remain the same: the propaganda describing each insurgency will picture what they term as an 'oppressed' people rising to overthrow the alleged oppressor. The objective—a communist dictatorship—will persist. . . . The insurgency environment is dynamic. The world has many dissatisfied people whom the communists can exploit in their quest for destruction of free society. This poses a threat that will be present for a long time."

The Special Action Force for Latin America, better known as the Green Berets, was formed in 1962 and located at Fort Gulick in the Panama Canal Zone. In addition to operating mobile training teams in Chile and elsewhere, the Green Berets have provided the tone and distinctive character of the training at Fort Gulick, both ideological and technical. The significance of this point is that the armed forces of Latin America, as already demonstrated in Brazil and Uruguay, and most recently in Chile, have taken on the characteristics of this special force rather than those of the peacetime armed forces of the United States. The distinction is vital. The green Berets do not see themselves as part of the regular army, but as a group with its own purposes and methods.

Organized in 1952 as a revival of the World War II OSS to fight the Cold War in Europe, the force was heavily European in its composition. A one-time member has described them as "self-consciously uprooted men, emotionally and intellectually detached from the mainstream of civilian society."[6] What was most striking about them, he added, was their ability to kill, without passion or the justifications of panic or crisis, anyone who presented an obstacle to the orderly conduct of an intelligence operation. "Such a clerkly impersonality about killing a prisoner has found a comparison in the administrative routine of the Nazi death camps, whose SS commanders would complain to one another about the bureaucratic difficulties of their task and compare notes on the technical and organizational solutions they had found most satisfactory." As they read the inside reports on the "administrative processes" which preceded and followed the attack on La Moneda on September 11, 1973, such instructors must have felt proud of their ability to pass on their knowledge and skills. During that period of testing, the career officers proved that they had fully internalized the values taught them in the barracks, foremost among which—according to Jonathan Kandell of the *New York Times*—are a virulent anti-marxism, a strong distrust of partisan politics, a puritanical morality, and a craving for unity and order.[7]

The distorted understanding of the role of the individual soldier and of the military institution which results from training in the Canal Zone has been noted by psychiatrists and social scientists in all parts of Latin America. Typical is the comment of a Chilean pastor who interviewed many

153

trainees in his professional work. "Their personality is deformed by an intensive brainwashing which equates all protest with communist conspiracies. There is also the brutalization which results from a regime that turns a civilized Chilean into an animal. Ours is a gentle country, without wild beasts, poisonous snakes or mosquitoes. Our men are unprepared for a training which includes extreme brain stresses, physical stresses, emotional stresses, electric shocks and so on. An average man becomes totally unbalanced. It is very hard to get him to a normal outlook."[8] With this comes a messiah complex, a conviction that the armed forces alone understand what is good for the country and that their leaders monopolize the country's skills and political wisdom. The 29,000 officers and enlisted men who have graduated from Fort Gulick include 170 who today are heads of government, cabinet ministers, commanding generals, chiefs of staff or directors of intelligence in Latin America. Six of them hold high positions in Chile's armed forces, as director of intelligence, and commanding officers of the Second Infantry Division and the Support Division at Santiago, the Third Infantry Division at Concepción, the Engineer School at Tejas Verdes, and the Paratroop and Special Forces School near Santiago.[9]

The three branches of the armed forces of Chile have a combined strength of 42,000 men: 23,000 in the army organized in twelve infantry regiments, eight artillery regiments, four horse cavalry regiments, and two armored regiments; 14,000 in the navy with three cruisers and 31 smaller ships; and 8,000 in the air force with 230 aircraft, including jets. Chile has compulsory military service, but there are many exceptions. About 20,000 are inducted each year for a 12-month stint, which leaves a hard core of 22,000 long-term officers and men. The 26,000 carabineros are all long-term. Organized on a military basis as an independent service, they constitute a second army.

The distinctive quality of the Chilean armed forces,

according to French sociologist Alain Joxe who recently studied them in depth, is not that they are apolitical but that—unlike their counterparts in other Latin American countries—they usually manage to play their role inconspicuously. Their nonintervention is "a latent and permanent participation in the political game, not a simple abstention." When they intervene, as in 1891 and from 1924 to 1931, they remodel the state to serve the upper and middle sectors and the bureaucracy. "One intervention in Chile is worth ten in other countries: it is perfect." [10] Ex-President Eduardo Frei and Cardinal Silva were apparently among the many who did not realize how this traditional self-understanding of the armed forces had been altered under Pentagon mentorship in recent years.

Like all previous presidents of Chile, Allende courted the armed forces. Before taking office, he agreed to a constitutional amendment which guaranteed that he would not interfere with their powers and privileges while president. He tried hard to convince them that the successful implementation of his programs would be to their benefit. "There are no powerful armed forces where there are people decimated by sickness or punished by lack of culture. There are no powerful armed forces in countries which are economically and culturally dependent." From the outset of his term, he included many military men in important administrative posts. A general was named head of the Chuquicamata Copper Company, and representatives of the three services were put on the national production boards of the copper, iron and nitrate companies, and also on the National Planning Organization.

Allende's opponents were not less assiduous. The United States wooed the Chilean armed forces openly by continuing a high level of aid to them when aid to all other Chileans was stopped. In October 1971, General Prats as commander-in-chief made an unprecedented appeal to politicians to stop meddling in the armed forces. [11] But the meddling continued. Five months later, the government announced that the Fatherland and Liberty movement had tried unsuccessfully to get elements of the military to join in a coup attempt.[12] Gradually three political positions formed within the armed forces. Some began to promote a Brazilian solution, a military take-over followed by a long period of open military dictatorship which would crush the popular structures developed during the UP tenure of office, even at the risk of a bitter civil war. A second group thought that the military would have to move, but that it should be a "golpe blanco" (white coup) which would simply involve a notification to the president that he would have to resign and leave the country, creating the need for a temporary caretaker government while new elections were being arranged. These were confident that the new president would be Eduardo Frei as head of the Christian Democrats, supported by the National Party. The third position in the armed forces was similar to Allende's own in the UP coalition, the need for literal maintenance of the constitution. That meant support for Allende as long as he functioned constitutionally. The main supporter of this view was General Prats, the commander-in-chief. [13]

The Right and the Left were equally agreed that the introduction of generals to top decision posts in the UP cabinet toward the end of 1972 would slow down the rate of implementation of the UP program to lead Chile toward socialism. As such, it was welcomed by moderates and opposed by extremists on both sides who believed confrontation was inevitable and should not be postponed. The differences extended even to the members of the UP coalition. The Communist Party, always concerned with maintaining the economy in good order while bringing it under state control and ownership, consistently welcomed moves that reduced tension without radically altering the direction of movement. A minority within the Socialist Party shared Allende's concern with maintaining constitutional forms and agreed with him that this step was unavoidable. The majority was more concerned not to lose the momentum, which was also the position of the two groups who had split off from the Christian Democrats earlier, MAPU and MIC. That view was held even more strongly by the MIR, which supported the UP in general terms without forming part of the coalition. These elements were happy when Prats left the cabinet in April 1973 to resume his post of commander-in-chief, a change which was widely interpreted as a show of confidence by the government in its ability to survive by itself, as a result of its excellent showing in the March elections. Allende's confidence of his ability to restrain the extremists was again shown a few days later when he adopted a hard line against MIR groups who were planning to seize private and state food-distribution centers.[14]

Relations of the government with the church showed new strains about the same time, when Cardinal Silva expressed grave concern about a program of school reform which the government announced it planned to implement right away. The approach adopted by the cardinal was interesting. Although it was clear that his substantive concern was that church-related schools might be adversely affected, he did not raise this issue. Neither did he challenge the substance of the proposed reforms, since all were long agreed that the existing curriculum was indefensible. Chile still maintained an arts-oriented education program which benefited only the small minority of students who went on to the university. It failed to prepare for their livelihood the vast majority of poor and lower-middle-class children who dropped out at the grade-school and high-school level. All the cardinal said publicly was that the education issue was so grave that it deserved a public debate. Instead of seeking justification for the changes in "old laws" which had never been implemented, which is what the government planned (as it had done successfully

157

for seizing businesses not being operated in the national interest), it should—he said—go to Congress for approval. To go to Congress was to ensure rejection of the proposal. It was a dilemma for Allende. After some hesitation and a private meeting with the cardinal, he decided to put the plan in cold storage. But even after he did, the opposition tried to get all the value they could out of the issue, organizing a big protest in Santiago by students representing the wealthy elements who benefited from the existing curriculum.

The escalation of polarization after the March elections was soon the major topic of discussion, blame being distributed according to the attitudes and prejudices of each. Marcel Niedergang reported in early April to *Le Monde* (Paris) that the shock troops of the Right, ordered some months earlier to suspend activities in hope of the electoral defeat of Allende, were loose again. The neo-fascist "Protecto" group had clashed with squatters in Santiago, two people being killed. Several premises belonging to the Socialist Party had been burned. About the same time, the London-based newsletter *Latin America* was suggesting that Washington was orchestrating the new offensive. Its negotiating team had hardened its line significantly in the debt negotiations talks in March, it said, insisting that Chile pay $700 million compensation for nationalized United States assets before it would even begin to discuss renegotiation of the old debts. Washington was also reported to be urging the Paris Club to take a stronger position than it had taken a year earlier, it said. And if the credit lines from the United States were not reopened promptly, the economic collapse could come soon. "At this point in time, the United States seems very much the villain of the piece," it summed up, adding that the opposition in Congress was also clearly pinning its hopes on an economic collapse in the next few months.

Justification indeed existed for such gloomy forecasts.

After more than two years with little capital investment or importation of spare parts, industry and transport were in a bad way. Inflation had reached crisis levels, with no end in sight. The opposition blamed the government policies; the government, the refusal of Congress to approve fiscal controls or to enable the government to suppress the black market. "The entire nation wonders anxiously whether Chile is engaged on an ineluctable course toward civil war," Pierre Kalfon reported to *Le Monde* at the beginning of May.[15]

Allende continued his long search for some understanding with the Christian Democrats which would enable him to work with Congress without abandoning the socialist program on which he had been elected. Eduardo Frei was intransigent. He told an Italian newspaper that there was no possibility of collaboration with Allende and his government, because they were "taking hesitant steps toward Marxist totalitarianism." But his party was not quite so clear. It indicated in April that it would not renew the alliance with the National Party in the Democratic Confederation when it expired on May 20. Many of its members feared they were losing their identity. Renán Fuentealba, the party chairman, said: "We must work to maintain alive the revolutionary alternatives proposed by Christian Democracy. We must also say clearly to Chile that, while we reject the state takeovers of UP, we never want to return to the position existing before."[16] To encourage this trend, Allende sharply criticized MIR's efforts to increase tension by seizing factories and organizing sit-ins in government food-distribution centers. In an address on radio and television, he urged workers not to take any notice of "the calls from the ultra-left adventurers who want to discredit the government."[17] The Right was understandably happy to exploit such differences. *El Mercurio* published what *Le Monde* described as "extravagant statements" praising the strikers at El Teniente copper

159

mine. The prospects of an understanding between the government and the Christian Democrats evaporated when, in circumstances which raised the suspicion that the shot had come from the Christian Democrat headquarters, a worker was killed in a demonstration. Shortly after, the possibility was finally laid to rest when the hard-liners in the Christian Democrat party elected Patricio Aylwin, a supporter of Frei, to succeed Fuentealba as chairman.

A critical point was reached in June when the National Party asserted that the Allende administration was "no longer legitimate." About a week later, the government announced it had discovered and squashed a planned coup. Just a day later, at eight o'clock in the morning of Friday June 29, the second armored tank regiment, led by Colonel Roberto Souper, headed for the presidential palace, La Moneda, in the center of Santiago, stopping for traffic lights on the way. Supported by armored cars and infantry, it surrounded the palace and opened fire on it. As soon as Allende learned at his home three miles away of the attack, he arranged to address the nation by radio. "In these difficult moments for Chile," he said, "the working class must demonstrate its willingness to fight as well as its sense of responsibility. It must not lose faith and should not allow itself to be massacred. But it must be more united than ever and must demonstrate to all that it is the major force behind the Chilean revolution." Meanwhile the right-wing Radio Agricultura was giving a different message to Chileans. "This is the situation right now at the presidential palace, where all the doors are closed and from which there is no sign of resistance. Tanks and other armed vehicles are surrounding the government palace in what is unquestionably a decisive action to carry out changes which the majority of the country demands." There were indications that Radio Agricultura knew in advance that a coup was imminent. At seven that morning it transmitted a message that sounded like a call to the military. If it was, there was no response. The tanks blasted away for an hour or longer, killing more than 20 people and wounding 40, but no general or admiral announced his support. Instead, General Prats, the commander-in-chief, put himself at the head of four regiments and the plotters fled down back streets where they were quickly isolated and forced to surrender. Pablo Rodriguez, leader of the fascist Fatherland and Freedom movement, and Benjamin Matte, former president of the National Agricultural Society, took refuge in the Ecuadorean embassy along with other top leaders of the plot.

Although a military fiasco, the attempt had serious political repercussions. At about 9:30 a.m., while the outcome was still uncertain, Allende called on the workers of Chile to occupy the factories in which they worked. This would serve as a warning to the hesitant military that they would have to deal not only with a handful of politicians but with the workers of the country prepared to fight. Factories in Santiago, Concepción and other cities were seized and the owners and managers were expelled. At noon, Allende spoke once more by radio, calling for a massive demonstration of support in front of the presidential palace at six that evening. Enormous crowds invaded Santiago from all directions, dressed for battle, a few with guns, but most with pitchforks, machetes, wrenches and clubs. The proponents of physical force were jubilant. The day had demonstrated, they claimed, that real power was now with the workers and they should use it. In a single blow, the area of the economy withdrawn from private ownership had been doubled. The seized factories, they urged, should never be returned.

That quickly became a prime issue when in mid-July rumors spread that Allende, under pressures from Frei, was preparing to give back some of the factories. Allende did, in fact, engage in protracted discussions with the Christian Democrats during July and August, and the seized fac-

161

tories figured large in them. The Christian Democrats wanted them back, but that was not all they wanted in return for support in Congress. They wanted Allende to sign the constitutional amendment rolling back the nationalizations without congressional approval, to take whatever action might be necessary to disband and disarm the paramilitary forces of both Right and Left, and to put generals in all key posts in the cabinet. In this way, they reasoned, Allende would be effectively neutralized, and the armed forces could run the country for the rest of his term without technical violation of the constitutional norms.

To pressure the government, the Confederation of Truck Owners in the last week of July renewed the work stoppage of the previous October. By this time, the paramilitary organization of the extreme Right, Fatherland and Freedom, was thoroughly organized and armed. It joined in a campaign of sabotage aimed at isolating Santiago from the countryside and the ports. Bridges, tunnels and power lines were dynamited. An oil pipeline was cut. After the October stoppage, 10,000 truck owners had left the 50,000-man Confederation to form a gremio that supported the government. When they tried to maintain operations, their trucks were sabotaged and their men attacked, and finally their president was assassinated. The government ruled the work stoppage seditious and authorized the seizure of idle trucks. The response was a series of sympathy strikes by doctors, lawyers, builders, teachers, nurses, store owners and various groups of white-collar workers organized in gremios which supported the policies of the Christian Democrats.

For the workers who had seized the factories, the issue of retaining them acquired the same primacy as did the drive to recover them for the other side. Many more defense councils of workers were created, and the areas around the factories were cordoned off and patrolled to prevent attacks by the rightist paramilitary groups or even occupation by the police. Everywhere people were reverting to their primary class loyalties. General elections in the labor movement a year earlier had revealed that more than three out of every four blue-collar workers favored pro-government trade unions. In the interval, the proportion had risen substantially, as had the level of commitment and class identification.

On August 8, as Fatherland and Freedom showered Santiago with leaflets calling for the violent overthrow of the government, Allende brought the heads of the three armed services and the head of the carabineros into the cabinet, saying this was "the last chance" to avoid civil war. The Christian Democrats said, however, that this was not enough. They now wanted an entirely military cabinet, with military men also at the intermediate levels of the administration. A few days later he offered to sign the constitutional reform measure giving Congress control of further nationalizations on two conditions. Congress must first reveal which of the seized factories would be returned to private ownership, and it must agree that a two-thirds majority is needed to override a presidential veto in the case of other important constitutional reforms. Again the Christian Democrats refused to compromise. They wanted a total victory and it would have to include the resignation of the under-secretary of Transport, Jaime Faivovich, the key figure in preventing a total collapse of the movement of food during the continuing truck stoppage.

Meanwhile, a change in the attitude of the armed forces was becoming steadily more obvious. A new law giving them power to search for illegally held arms was being used almost exclusively against the workers in occupied factories, while the paramilitary forces of the Right were being overlooked in their sabotage campaigns. A particularly provocative operation was the dynamiting of a pylon as Allende began a radio and television address to the nation on the truck stoppage. It cut all power to the city and province of Santiago and prevented the broadcast. It also quickly became clear that the head of the air force, General Cesar Ruiz, was making less than wholehearted efforts to end the truck stoppage. On August 19, Allende dropped Ruiz from the cabinet, at the same time accepting the resignation of Faivovich as a concession to the Christian Democrats. Ruiz said he had been unable to perform the tasks assigned to him as cabinet minister because his requests were not complied with, requests understood to include the bringing in of other officers to form a chain of command under him. Allende simultaneously dropped Ruiz as air force chief, an action which brought into the open some of the new trends developing within the armed forces. The air force went on an alert, explained by its spokesman as "a demand for the recognition as the only authentic commander-in-chief of the air force of the man who loyally and honorably represents that institution, General Cesar Ruiz." The wives of generals and other high-ranking officers began protest demonstrations outside the home of General Prats and delivered a letter to him calling on him to resign.

Meanwhile, Congress was fanning the flames with a series of actions designed to delegitimize the administration. On August 23, the Chamber of Deputies passed a resolution calling on the armed forces to compel the President "to govern within the law." The government, it said, had repeatedly broken the law, and the constitution had suffered "a grave collapse," making it the duty of the armed forces to re-establish order throughout the country. Rightist gangs provoked street fighting in Santiago, and the Central Labor Confederation ordered workers to remain in the factories at night in order to prevent "the impending fascist coup." That the description of "fascist" applied by the workers to the opposition was more than a slogan was shown by a number of incidents. The editor in charge of *El Mercurio* during Augustin Edwards' self-imposed exile in the United States admitted under questioning that he was a former Nazi. The opposition press developed a hate campaign against foreigners, with strong anti-Semitic over-tones. *La Prensa*, organ of the Christian Democrats, said Chile had been taken over by a Jewish-Communist cell. Its headline read: "Chile, Jewish Communism; Russia, Anti-Jewish Communism." The entire Jewish community in Chile numbers only 25,000.[18] References to the Night of the Long Knives of Hitler's Germany were frequent, and the favorite slogan on the walls of Santiago's buildings was the single word *Djakarta*, a call to the military to liquidate the communists in the same way as 300,000 to 400,000 Indonesians had been massacred in an anti-communist drive in 1966. Historians of the transfer of knowhow will note that the proposal of a Jakarta solution in Chile was first made in an internal memorandum of a United States transnational company in 1970.

In the midst of this atmosphere of conflict, General Prats requested and was refused a vote of confidence from his general staff. Believing that wholesale dismissal of generals would precipitate a coup, Prats resigned both as minister and as head of the armed forces. He was succeeded in the latter post by General Augusto Pinochet Ugarte. The result was further polarization. Worker defense committees continued to spread, emerging as rank-and-file organizations able to mobilize sectors of the work force never reached by the organized trade union movement. They had sprung up in Concepción and in the far south, a process not particularly welcomed by the Communist Party which still sought compromise and believed in leadership from above. Right-wing terrorist activity also accelerated. The rightists within the Christian Democrats openly joined the National Party in urging Allende to resign. A smaller group of Christian Democrats headed by Radomiro Tomic, the party's candidate in the 1970 presidential elections, not only rejected this move but threatened to split the party by insisting that Congress also had to make concessions. It would be as reasonable for the President to ask the military to control Congress, Tomic said, as it was for Congress to ask the military to control the President. But the din from both sides drowned out such voices of reason in the middle.

7.

The Generals Revolt

Before the overt move to destroy the constitutional system and end the Allende administration, the armed forces had to be purged. One of the few strict constitutionalists in the upper ranks had already been eliminated with the assassination of General René Schneider in 1970. The resignation of his successor as commander-in-chief, General Carlos Prats, in the belief that thus he could avoid a military takeover, left control with generals and admirals whose commitment to the privileges of their class took precedence over their tradition of noninterference and their oaths of office. But how about the lower officers and the ranks whose class identification was mostly with the UP government? It was by no means evident that an emotional gap had been opened between them and the workers. On the contrary, the mass demonstrations that followed the aborted tank attack on the presidential palace on June 29 had hailed the soldiers as the protectors of the people's rights, the marchers chanting a rhymed slogan: *Soldado, amigo, el pueblo está contigo* (Soldier, friend, the people are with you).

A hint of the methods being used inside the armed services to test the reliability of the men came to light on September 5 when spokesmen for the parties forming the UP coalition charged that the navy was imprisoning and torturing leftist marines. An incident about a month earlier, which had then been described as an aborted coup, was now interpreted as actually a "false coup," an exercise to determine which men would join and which would not. Since that time, it was charged, more than 100 judged unreliable had been imprisoned and "cruelly tortured."[1] Meanwhile, the other services were also making up their lists of unreliables. Military unity, it became known later, was bought at the cost of considerable bloodshed within the armed forces, blood shed coldbloodedly. "According to well-informed persons now leaving Santiago," *Latin America* newsweekly reported two months later, "several hundred officers who were thought likely to oppose the takeover were shot on the night of September 10-11. . . . Some sources speak of between 2,000 and 3,000 members of the armed forces and police losing their lives in the coup before the coup."[2]

From the beginning of September, the armed forces were engaged in constant searches for arms in factories occupied by the workers since the June 29 tank attack on the presidential palace. Apparently the plotters had been convinced by their own propaganda that the workers were heavily armed, and they also anticipated that General Prats might rally a substantial part of the armed forces to support the constitution. Brazil reportedly made contingency plans for a civil war in Chile, with pro-Allende forces aided by Argentina and a diversion into Paraguay by exiles in Argentina. Brazil's army minister assured the ambassador of Paraguay to Brazil in the presence of newsmen that Brazil would come to the military aid of his country if invaded.[3] In response to the build-up of the militia of the right-wing Fatherland and Freedom movement, workers did try to accumulate arms to defend the factories, but the quantities were nominal. Early in September, the Opposition press secured and published an internal report of the militant leftist MIR. It dealt with logistics in Concepción, the birthplace of MIR and its reputed stronghold. In this city of 600,000, it had 300 to 400 active militants armed with a total of 20 rifles, 20 pistols, and a stock of hand grenades.[4] Nevertheless, the search continued. On September 8, air force troops opened fire on a factory occupied by workers. The same day brought reports of a farm worker who died as a result of tortures applied by troops searching for arms, and of another who was suspended for an hour from a helicopter in an effort to get information from him. "The military coup is already under way, and the workers must mobilize to stop it," said Jaime Faivovich, the former under-secretary of Transport.[5]

At the nearest United States air force base at Mendoza, Argentina, little more than 100 miles northeast of Santiago, military activity had been reported up during July and August, as it had been during the earlier preparations for violent overthrow of the Chilean government in October 1972. Twenty-two airplanes of the United States air force were located there during the second week of September. One of these was WB57, license number 631-3298, the weather model of the spy plane RB57, and according to a Buenos Aires news agency, it played "a central role in coordinating communications for the Chilean armed forces" when they moved to overthrow the government. United States authorities admit that it flew four missions between September 7 and September 12 to coordinate "weather programming with the Argentine government," but insist that it did not violate Chilean air space. Such violation would not be necessary to perform the function of coordinating communications between the various air force, army and navy bases in Chile. A similar function of coordinating communications on the various battle fronts was performed during the Vietnam War by United States planes flying from Udorn, Thailand.[6]

On September 10, Charles Horman went from Santiago to Viña del Mar, a seaside resort close to the naval base of Valparaiso. A United States citizen, Horman had been in Chile for some months, working on a documentary film. At the Miramar Hotel, where he stayed, Horman met some Americans, and he later told his wife that some of them had spoken frankly and perhaps carelessly to him about their reasons for being where they were. They included a Captain Ray E. Davis, U.S. Navy, Lieutenant-Colonel Patrick Ryan, U.S. Army, both attached to the U.S. Embassy in Santiago, and a retired naval engineer named Arthur Crater. Ryan, who had been nine months in Chile after three tours in Vietnam, told Horman he had taken a Chilean naval officer to the United States on a million-dollar shopping spree for equipment the previous month. On September 14, he reported that between 1,500 and 3,000 had been killed by the Chilean military, because "they're doing search-and-destroy missions like in Vietnam." Crater was a little less specific about his concerns. All he confided was that he had arrived from Panama on September 6 "to do a job with the navy." Horman suspected he knew what that job was when several United States naval officers and other military personnel who were also in the hotel boasted to him of "the smooth operation" which the revolt proved to be.

Valparaiso was where the navy began the revolt early on the morning of September 11. Just after 6 that morning, Allende was notified by police officers at his residence that military forces of three regiments were advancing upon La Moneda, the presidential palace in the center of Santiago. He immediately went there, and at about 8:30 he announced that Valparaiso had been seized by naval forces, and that he was awaiting a decision from the army to support the government. He would, he said, defend La Moneda and the people's right to a democratic government to the end. Meanwhile, the military were moving into position in all areas. They sealed off the borders and the airports and took control of all public and private communications and transportation. Government radio stations were machine-gunned from the air and ordered to stop transmitting. Two of them, Portales and Magallanes, continued to transmit and carried a further message from Allende at 9:30. At this time, also, the trade union federation (CUT) called for a general strike and ordered all workers to go on a total alert in their factories. Shortly afterward, tanks opened fire on La Moneda, and the radio stations held by the military issued an ultimatum that the air force would bomb La Moneda at 11 if it refused to surrender. The women, including Allende's two daughters, were allowed to leave, and just after 11 o'clock the jets dropped seventeen bombs and gutted the palace. A tank broke down the door and troops fought their way in. By the time the last resistance was overcome, Allende was dead. The generals reported that he had committed suicide, but a member of his personal guard who escaped said he was killed by a burst of machinegun fire in hand-to-hand fighting.[7]

The four signatories of the ultimatum to Allende described themselves as the heads of the four armed forces, General Augusto Pinochet Ugarte for the army, General Gustavo Leigh Guzmán for the air force, Admiral José Toribio Merino Castro for the navy, and General Cesar Mendoza Frank for the carabineros. The heads of the navy and carabineros were self-appointed, revealing that the commanders named by Allende, Admiral Montero and General Sepúlveda, had been unwilling to join the revolt.[8] The four established themselves as a Junta headed by Pinochet, proclaimed martial law, ordered immediate surrender of all arms, with resisters or anyone carrying arms to be shot on sight, abrogated the constitution and abolished Congress. All newspapers were suppressed except *El Mercurio* and *La Tercera*.

171

Simultaneously with the attack on La Moneda, the military began an all-out offensive against the workers who in response to Allende's call had mobilized in their factories. These were attacked by tanks and bombed from the air. A 24-hour curfew was proclaimed in Santiago, and all night the airplanes and helicopters circled, while explosions rocked the industrial sectors. Within a few days, all organized resistance throughout the country was ended, with loss of life estimated as high as 25,000. Meanwhile all foreigners were ordered to report to the authorities, as well as many Chileans identified by name. The first list included all the leaders of the Allende government, all congressmen belonging to the parties of the UP coalition and leaders of these parties. The few who gave themselves up were sent to internment on Dawson Island in Tierra del Fuego. Those who managed to escape the search parties sought asylum in friendly embassies.

A systematic search for suspects followed in factories, offices and homes. The Junta intensified a theme started more than a month earlier which blamed foreigners for all of Chile's sufferings, charging that the UP government had brought in 10-15,000 gangsters and murderers who were killing Chileans and wrecking the economy. The national stadium in Santiago became the main collection center for suspects, holding at times as many as ten thousand. From there, they were sent to prison camps in various parts of the country and to islands off the coast. Calls to report all suspects to the authorities were broadcast endlessly on the radio, and big rewards were offered for identified leaders.

Not surprisingly, the Christian Democrats divided immediately. Eduardo Frei and the right wing of the party expressed approval, Frei apparently hoping that the Junta would follow the constitutional procedures and pass the presidency to him as head of the Senate. Twelve Christian Democrat congressmen, including Bernardo Leighton, Renán Fuentealba, Fernando Sanhueza and Ignacio Palma, promptly disassociated themselves from Frei and categorically condemned the revolt and seizure of power. Challenging the claim made by Patricio Aylwin, leader of the Christian Democrat party, that the military takeover was "a necessary pre-emptive action," they blamed the far left and far right for having created "the false impression" that a coup was unavoidable. When it became clear that the Junta had no intention of relinquishing power but was rather committed to rule Chile dictatorially for the indefinite future, the enthusiasm of Frei and his associates understandably waned. Aylwin said at a news conference that the Christian Democrats do not accept directives regarding change of the constitution that do not come from the people, this in response to an indication from the Junta that it would promulgate a new constitution by decree, Brazilian style. Aylwin also deplored the outlawing of marxist parties.[9]

The Catholic and Protestant churches issued parallel statements, that of the Protestants fractionally more chilly than that of the Catholics. Both recognized the fact of the take-over, hoped there would be no reprisals, urged cooperation of all Chileans with the new regime. In a press interview, Cardinal Silva attempted to formulate a totally non-political stand, abstracting from the realities of church-state relations in Chile and throughout Latin America. "The church is not called on to form governments or to overthrow them, to recognize them or not to recognize them. We accept the government which these people have chosen to give themselves, and we serve it." The Cardinal was more realistic when invited by the Junta to preside in the cathedral at a *Te Deum* of thanksgiving on the National Day (September 18). He compromised by arranging a Mass for the Fallen in a less conspicuous church. But even this compromise was widely condemned. The British Broadcasting Corporation expressed a general world reaction in its report: "While the bishops, wealthy landowners and Junta members are in church praying for peace, the ordinary soldier is fighting in the streets and taking the factories from the poor." The views of progressive Christians throughout Latin America were formulated by Argentina's Third World Movement. It affirmed solidarity with the Chilean workers and people, noting that participation in a process of liberation inevitably brings a profound reaction "which the Bible calls anti-Christ," and which expressed itself for all to see "in the massacre perpetrated on the Chilean people without mercy under the apostate appeal to Christian values and to God." The forces of imperialism, it said, are moving to slow down the process of liberation for Chile and for all Latin America, but "we repudiate this oppression, proclaim once more our identification with the people of Chile and our gratitude to President Allende for his leadership."

When Pope Paul publicly deplored the "violent acts of repression" in Chile, Silva reportedly said the Pope must have been misinformed, blaming foreign priests and nuns who had been expelled by the Junta as one of the sources of the misinformation. This charge was immediately contradicted by 100 priests and nuns in Chile, two-thirds of them Chileans. They wrote the Pope that he was indeed well informed "regarding the sad situation which the oppressed and repressed of Chile are currently enduring, with the very poor and foreigners being ill-treated, a situation of which we ourselves are witnesses." Nor was Silva's intervention more favorably received when in late October he visited the bishops of the United States, Canada and Western Europe, and also the Pope. His purpose was spiritual, not political, he said, but sources close to the Junta insisted that it had persuaded him to make the trip. He reportedly urged the bishops and Pope Paul to de-emphasize the violations of human rights in Chile. In this way, he would have more leverage to promote a quick return to civilian rule, presumably under the leadership of his friend,

Eduardo Frei. Among the criticisms, nevertheless, there were some words of comfort for Silva. Mrs. Allende, the President's widow, was in Rome while he was there, and her response to newsmen was: "Cardinal Silva Henriquez devoted himself constantly—just as Salvador Allende did—to avoiding civil war, and we all know how much he did to prevent it." And an underground newsletter produced in Chile by opponents of the Junta—North Americans, to judge from internal evidence—recognizes the difficulty of the choices he has to make. "A subtle passive resistance could at best describe his manner as he courts the members of the Junta and still provides assistance for some of Chile's still wanted persons."[10]

The attitude of some of Silva's close associates is reflected in a confidential report sent in October by Caritas-Chile, the official welfare organization of the Church in Chile, to International Caritas in Switzerland and the national organizations in all parts of the world. Having referred to "the magnitude of chaos in which the country finds itself after three years of inefficiency, corruption and hatred," it comments: "Anyone who has observed—and some time participated or has been forced to live—the carnival-like event of the Regime of the so-called experience of the Chilean route toward socialism, through the scientific and unique system of marxism, at this moment feels the sensation of leaving the orchestra seat with the bitterness of the one who has been forced to see the long-scope picture (3 years), 'Promises, Love and Deceit.' " The document continues in the same strain, misrepresentation of and contempt for the UP regime, admiration for the self-sacrificing generals who "with professional honesty" have made the sacrifice needed to eliminate hatred and restore the rule of love and justice in Chile.[11] Just how many in the Church's organizations think in such terms is still impossible to determine. What is clear is that most of those who do not are keeping a low profile. "The only vocal resistance of the Catholic Church is that of the Archbishop of Puerto Montt [Alberto Rencoret Donoso] in defense of a persecuted French priest," reports the underground newsletter. "He said that the marxist literature in the priest's possession was 'something any respectable library would have,' and that his organization of the poor and work with JAP [state food rationing program] was 'necessary.' " The Archbishop, it further reported, had expressed his response to the revolt by leaving his comfortable home and taking up residence in a small wooden structure (known locally as a *media agua*) in a poor neighborhood.[12]

Particular efforts were made to prevent the outside world from getting accurate information about the situation. All dispatches were heavily censored, and the movement of correspondents in the country was restricted. Four foreign correspondents were expelled, including the representative of *Le Monde*, the newspaper which had consistently given the most accurate and informed accounts of events during the previous three years. All borders were closed for a week and international communications cut. Massive cleanups were carried out to conceal signs of massacres before the first newsmen were allowed in on September 19. They were also carefully shepherded under the watchful eye of the Junta's press attaché, Federico Willoughby, formerly an employee of the United States Information Service and of the Ford Motor Company. Oldrich Haselman, representative of the UN's High Commissioner for Refugees, was forced to wait in Buenos Aires until September 20, and the International Red Cross was held up even longer.

One of the first eyewitness accounts was that of John Barnes of *Newsweek* who smuggled himself into the Santiago city morgue one day toward the end of September. "One hundred and fifty dead bodies were laid out on the ground floor, awaiting identification by family members.

Upstairs, I passed through a swinging door and there in a dimly lighted corridor lay at least 50 more bodies, squeezed one against another, their heads propped up against the wall. They were all naked. Most had been shot at close range under the chin. Some had been machine-gunned in the body. . . . They were all young and, judging from the roughness of their hands, all from the working class. A couple of them were girls, distinguishable among the massed bodies only by the curves of their breasts. Most of their heads had been crushed. . . . I was able to obtain an official morgue body-count from the daughter of a member of the staff: by the fourteenth day following the coup, she said, the morgue had received and processed 2,796 corpses."[13]

Faithful to the teaching they had received in their training at various academies conducted by the Pentagon in the United States and the Panama Canal Zone, the members of the Junta identified "the foreign mercenaries of marxism" as the cause of all of Chile's problems, and they concentrated on extirpating this "cancer" from the country. A first step was an orgy of book burning such as the world had not known since Hitler's Germany. Book-stores were ransacked and all books and magazines that had any hint of left-leaning were destroyed. A long list of publications was prepared which it was declared illegal to possess, these including the classic works of Marx and similar works. In the house-to-house searches the soldiers gathered up books and papers and tossed them from the windows to burn in the streets.

A coordinated program to weed out all members of the professional classes whose loyalty was in any way suspect was put into operation. A dossier was prepared in the archives of the information services of the armed forces on every doctor, lawyer, teacher, engineer and administrator in the country, and those on whom evidence of sympathy for the UP regime was developed were sacked or demoted.

Singled out for special punishment were the doctors and lawyers who had protested against the strike called in August 1973 as part of the campaign of economic chaos. They had accused strikers of unethical behavior for leaving the free clinics unmanned while they continued their private practice at home. Press advertisements called on all doctors and dentists who had failed to obey the strike order to submit their explanation in writing within 15 days under penalty of suspension.[14]

The loss of constitutional rights extended to the universities. As generally in Latin America, universities in Chile were largely self-regulating institutions. Students and professors elected the rector and the governing body through a weighted system of votes. Only in extreme circumstances were outside law officers invited or allowed to come on campus. All that is ended. Eduardo Boeninger, the Christian Democrat rector of the national university, offered his resignation in protest against the military assaults on the university buildings and the imprisonment of hundreds of professors. The Junta immediately accepted and put a general in his place. The elected rectors of the other universities and institutes of higher learning in the country, both state and private, were replaced by military men. A massive purge of professors and students followed, with a "prosecutor" named in each institution to receive written or oral denunciations of suspects and to expel those he judged unfit without giving them an opportunity to confront their accusers. Some graduate departments, particularly in the social sciences, have been closed indefinitely. A professor from Oxford, England, who was teaching at the Austral University, estimated that half the staff of the University of Concepción was being fired, and almost the entire staff of the Pedagogical Institute and of the School of Science of the University of Chile, both in Santiago. His estimate of the number killed at the Technical University, the first building attacked by the armed forces in Santiago as they were moving to oust the Allende government, was between 200 and 585.[15]

In spite of the Junta's efforts to conceal the terror, the broad outlines soon became apparent. The main spotlight was directed on the stadium in Santiago, the first staging point for prisoners. Some of the horrors of the week after the army revolt were described by Adam and Pat Garrett-Schesch to a subcommittee of the United States Senate. These two United States citizens, husband and wife, were in Chile to do research for their doctorates, Adam in history and Pat in sociology. They were held incommunicado in the stadium from September 14, a Friday, to September 21. Their evidence dealt with their experiences and observations. It has been corroborated in its overall thrust by many eyewitnesses.

"We witnessed and heard in the following manner between 400 and 500 executions by automatic weapons of people brought out in groups of ten to twenty.

"The most vivid experience was on Saturday, September 15, when we were still separated. Pat, located on the diagram (presented at the hearing) along near the exit to the football field, was sitting on a low wall waiting for interrogation. Glancing toward the intersection between the two wings, she saw a young man led out to the intersection by a guard. They paused, and the guard lit him a cigarette. He was then led into the field. From our wing, another person was led by and out. Within a couple of minutes, the group outside began singing. At this point, heavy automatic weapons fire began. As the firing continued, fewer and fewer people continued singing. Finally, the singing stopped and the continuous firing stopped, too. Immediately afterwards, a soldier returned and said to another guard standing a few feet from Patricia: 'There were thirty-seven people in that group.'

"One by one, prisoners would be brought, usually from short interviews in room number four, to the re-situation booth. After short paperwork, they would be put into one of two lines. One line toward the outside wall would be composed of people who were given back their personal documents and possessions. They were usually allowed to leave their arms at their sides. This line was unguarded. The second line would be formed with the prisoners under heavy guard—two or three soldiers with semi-automatic rifles with an armed officer for from 10-20 prisoners. Their arms would always be behind their backs or head. As soon as this line was complete, a noncommissioned officer would go to the cell-locker rooms 2, 3, 5, 6, 7, and turn on the exhaust fans if they were not already on. Immediately afterwards, the line would be led out. Within a few minutes from outside the hall in the stadium itself, we would hear a heavy sustained outburst of automatic weapons fire. None of the people in these lines ever returned, and the pattern was always the same. From late Saturday afternoon through Tuesday evening a total of more than 400 people were led out in this fashion."[16]

The Garrett-Schesches also reported that many people—including Adam—were beaten during interrogation. "We witnessed several different kinds of beating. . . . People were beaten into what the guards thought was the correct position when they were put against the wall to wait. People were severely beaten during interrogation—Adam saw one middle-aged man whose face was a bloody mess. Women and old people were beaten, too. . . . The degree of the beating ranged from Adam's case—mild—to so severe that the victims could only crawl on the floor. We watched a teenage boy being prodded by a guard to crawl to the water pipe coming out of the floor in order to get a drink of water."

In subsequent weeks, the interrogation techniques were refined to correspond with what has become standard operating procedure in much of the world since World War II, in Korea, Vietnam, Northern Ireland, Greece, Dominican Republic, Brazil, Uruguay, in all cases using techniques developed and propagated by the Pentagon. An underground newsletter from Chile in November 1973 summarizes the processes: "Tortures: psychological, solitary confinement, starvation, beating, cigarette burns, electric shock to genitals and down the inside of the throat, kicking, cutting off flesh with bayonets, rape, pulling finger nails." To which it adds the ominous footnote that torture "seems to have increased in the past few weeks."[17]

While most news reports dwelt mainly on conditions in Santiago and its neighborhood, the entire country was equally affected. A "Letter from the South" in the underground newsletter sums up the situation. "The workers and the poor are afraid. . . . The purge has begun. . . . The local pen is crowded, also the local regiment (barracks) and a recently completed hospital. . . . Here, as in all Chile, the unions practically don't exist any more." The Mapuche Indians, it continued, were being denounced by those who have taken their land, including a community of Franciscan priests to whom they had given ten acres of land for their house and who had expanded their holding to over 200 acres simply by seizing and enclosing adjoining Indian land. The Mapuches accused of being extremists were taken to the police station at Nueva Imperial in Cautín province, where they were detained without food, were given electric shocks through their testicles, had their heads shaven, while blindfolded all the time. After fifteen days of torture, they were removed to the prison at Temuco and the torture started all over again. " 'We are full of Marxist Indians,' the police say." Three hundred students, 90 percent of them Mapuches, and many in their final year, were expelled from the State Technical University of Temuco.[18]

The persistence of the organized terror was confirmed by an investigative team sent to Chile by the International Federation for the Rights of Man, the International Move-

181

ment of Catholic Lawyers, and the International Association of Democratic Lawyers. It reported as follows on its return to Geneva, October 17:

"Every day, even the eve of our departure from Santiago, bodies were taken from the River Mapocho, or left in the morgue or buried in common graves, or left to be decomposed where they had been killed, for the purpose of increasing the terror. The press every day reported prisoners killed 'attempting to escape.' After October 13, any mention of the number of persons executed, other than official statistics, was prohibited.

"The bodies showed grave mutilations. Most of the people detained, who are thousands in Santiago, have been tortured and ill-treated. Now before being set free, every prisoner has to make a declaration that he was not ill-treated.

"The persecution concentrates on foreigners. Propaganda against foreigners has become a state doctrine. Thousands of political refugees who could not get asylum are living in open fields and their situation is very precarious.

"The sacking of Pablo Neruda's home is only an illustration of the generalized practice. The laboratories of the Technical University of Santiago and of scientific institutes in Valparaiso have also been sacked.

"To the burning of libraries and of works which were regarded as seditious has followed the official prohibition of works by such authors as Jack London, Dostoevsky and Thomas Mann, among others. Various social science chairs have been suppressed and many professors have been suspended.

"The freedom of expression, of association, of assembly and of union action have been subjected to legal restrictions with criminal penalties for their violation. In many cases the functioning of ordinary justice has been suspended. The state of siege is being converted into a state of 'internal war,' regulated by rules which have recently been promulgated and which include new types of crime, heavier penalties, and the application of military courts which make their decisions behind closed doors by summary procedure, decisions which are immediately carried out.

"The official denials regarding violence committed against persons or the seizure of their goods are proved to be false by information and trustworthy accounts given to the members of the mission, as well as by the checking they themselves carried out personally."

For the record, official Washington admitted advance knowledge of the revolt of the generals but insisted it was not involved in any way. William E. Colby, head of the CIA, and Frederick Dixon Davis, one of his assistants, had a somewhat different story for a closed meeting of the House Committee on Inter-American Affairs. Colby was "the architect of the Phoenix program of political assassination and midnight arrest in Vietnam," in the words of Washington political commentator Nicholas von Hoffman, who says he spends six billion dollars a year of public funds for which there is no public accounting. When questioned on support of anti-Allende forces by United States corporations and Brazilian subsidiaries, they gave "equivocal answers." Davis said there was evidence of cooperation of business associations and chambers of commerce in Brazil with those in Chile, and that "there is funding and cooperation among groups with similar outlooks in other Latin American countries." They also admitted that the CIA between October 1970 and September 1973 had "penetrated" all Chilean political parties, had supported demonstrations against the Allende regime, had financed the opposition press, and had adopted a hard line in the financial negotiations between Washington and Santiago in late 1972 and early 1973. Because its reports indicated that the economic situation of Chile was in fact "deteriorating," it urged the White House to rebuff Allende's efforts to work out a settlement of the compensation issues and renegotiation of debts. Nixon accepted its advice, refusing even humanitarian help to Chile. For example, he turned down a request for credits to buy urgently needed wheat a week before the generals revolted, a request granted a few weeks later to the Junta. Colby also drew a grim picture of the Junta's repression. "Armed opposition now appears to be confined to sporadic, isolated attacks on security forces," he said, "but the regime believes that the Left is regrouping for coordinated sabotage and guerrilla activity," and it "is probably right in believing that its opponents have not been fully neutralized."[19]

The American public reacted cynically to Washington's claim to have remained uninvolved. Senator Fulbright, chairman of the Foreign Relations Committee of the United States Senate, said that his committee had received thousands of telegrams, letters and telephone calls. That, he said, was not unprecedented, but "what is unprecedented is their unanimity. Not one expresses approval, or even acceptance, of the coup. On the contrary, they express dismay, strong suspicions of United States involvement, and deep concern over the fate of Chilean supporters of the Allende regime and of the foreign exile community in Chile. They indicate a depth of public feeling which should be taken into account, both in Washington and Santiago.[20] "

President Juan Perón of Argentina expressed the almost universal belief and reaction of Latin Americans when asked if the United States had overthrown Allende. "I can't prove it, but I firmly believe it." Many Latin American countries proclaimed national days of mourning, and everywhere there were demonstrations against the United States. The ITT office in Barcelona, Venezuela, was bombed. Molotov cocktails were tossed at the United States embassy in Honduras. In Peru, the government-owned *Expreso* described the revolt as "a triumph for the CIA." An office of the First National City Bank in Buenos

Aires was set on fire. The *Christian Science Monitor* summed up hemispheric reaction by saying that Allende was being hailed as "a democratic martyr sacrificed to the United States" all through Latin America. Throughout Europe, popular reaction similarly zeroed in on the United States. ITT offices in Rome, Zurich and Madrid were bombed. Demonstrations in many cities against United States embassies and business offices brought clashes with police. "Down with the murderers and the CIA" read the banners behind which thousands marched through Paris. Twenty thousand protestors assembled in London in the biggest demonstration since the 1968 denunciations of the United States involvement in Vietnam. In an unprecedented break with tradition, the University of Brussels conferred an honorary doctorate on Allende posthumously as "a symbol of an ideal of political democracy" whose views are shared "by all members of the university community."

Perhaps most surprising of all was the aspect noted by Senator Fulbright, the depth, intensity and unanimity of reaction within the United States. Americans traditionally left foreign policy to the Administration. Even when the Brazilian military overthrew the constitutional government with close cooperation of the United States in 1964 and when the following year United States marines went into the Dominican Republic to block the return of the elected president, only small isolated groups expressed their dismay. In the interval, many people have come to the conclusion that this country with seven percent of the world's population is able to consume nearly half of the world's production only because the United States government and big business use their power to siphon off an unconscionable part of the wealth produced in poor countries like Chile. On September 11, within hours of the revolt, hundreds of Americans protested in front of the United Nations in New York. The weeks and months that followed were filled with rallies of solidarity for the people of Chile, teach-ins and strategy meetings. An International Week of Solidarity with Chile in October saw activities in 35 United States cities. Scores of magazines on college campuses and house organs of political and religious groups undertook a major and continuing involvement, forcing the Nixon Administration to take elaborate efforts to downgrade the Chile issue and specifically to pressure Congress to abandon plans for holding hearings on it. In spite of these White House efforts, the verdict of the Committee for Peace and Justice of the Association of Chicago Priests continues to express the view of the protesting groups. "Nixon is about as innocent in Chile as he was in the last presidential campaign here; Chile is Watergate with a passport."

Of particular concern to groups in the United States is the evidence that has gradually accumulated that the United States Embassy and Consulate in Santiago were staffed with ideological enemies of the Allende government, and that these failed to give United States citizens whom they suspected of sympathy with that regime the protection to which they were entitled, and perhaps even passed information about them to the Junta.

Here the most documented case is that of Charles Horman, who was in Viña del Mar when the revolt occurred and received the indiscreet revelations of what United States military and naval personnel were doing in nearby Valparaiso. On September 15, Captain Ray Davis gave him a ride back to Santiago, where he joined his wife. Two days later, in view of the continuing fighting in Santiago and the martial law, he went to the United States Embassy to ask protection for his wife and himself. Embassy officials said there was little they could do for him, and he returned home. Two hours later, he was arrested. His wife had gone into town and was caught there by the early curfew. She got home the following morning to find the house ransacked. She immediately notified the Consulate that her husband was missing. The Consulate did in fact have information that day that a body identified by the Chilean military as that of Charles Horman was in the morgue, but for an entire month it would not give his wife or family any clues as to his fate.

Two other United States citizens, Frank Teruggi and David Hathaway were arrested in the late evening of September 20. The Consulate was informed at 8 o'clock the following morning. As Hathaway later testified, Teruggi and he were both then in the stadium. At 6 o'clock that evening, Teruggi was removed, and the following evening his body was also in the morgue.

Richard Fagen, a Stanford University professor who had been in Chile earlier as a social science consultant to the Ford Foundation and knew all three, learned from friends that they were missing and went to the State Department, which indicated that the Embassy had not told it anything about them. He notified their families and pressure was brought through Congressmen on the State Department. Hathaway was quickly released and repatriated, and the deaths of the other two were confirmed. Fagen subsequently stated that Frederick Purdy, United States Consul in Santiago, had been positively identified to him by career embassy officials as a CIA agent, and one of them had said to him during the summer of 1972 that Purdy's "double loyalties" would pose great problems to United States citizens in Chile in the event of a coup. He also said that while he was in Chile, he had heard embassy and consular officials publicly, in diplomatic circles, labeling certain fellow-Americans as "traitorous," "communist" or "fellow traveler."[21]

Many other observers on the spot have confirmed the partisan attitude of the United States Embassy in Santiago. When other embassies were overflowing with political refugees, particularly that of Sweden whose heroic ambassador saved countless lives at the risk of his own, the United States refused all appeals. "The doors of the American Embassy are closed," reports the underground newsletter. "Our Embassy will not assist one single person. We know of a North American priest who was a naturalized Chilean in need of asylum. The North American Embassy said no."[22]

A young American woman from Madison, Wisconsin, with a two-year-old baby, went to the United States Embassy for help, and was there told to go to the Chilean police. Instead, she went to the Swedish Embassy and there she was given asylum.[23]

Ignoring all appeals and criticisms, Washington went grimly ahead with its program, obviously carefully planned well in advance, to reintegrate Chile into its sphere of influence. The flamboyant directness of Johnson's wheelings and dealing with the Brazilian generals in 1964 had been replaced by Nixon's low-profile deviousness. While private enterprise moved back directly, with lines of credit from the banks and promises of new investment from the industrialists, the first "aid" was not directly from Washington, but a massive loan supplied indirectly through its Latin American viceroy, Brazil. Within months, the strategy took substantial shape. A harsh price was going to be extracted from Chile's workers and peasants in return for their brief moment of dignity.

8.

The Brazilianization
of Chile

Salvador Allende's contribution to the history of Chile can be assessed from many viewpoints. As a politician pursuing unconventional objectives by conventional means, he had few peers. Even when his overwhelmingly powerful enemies in Congress abandoned the role of a loyal opposition, without which representational democracy cannot function, and when the judiciary dropped its mask of objectivity to become an integral part with Congress of the openly disloyal opposition, he refused consistently to play by their rules. He created no apparatus of secret police to harass his opponents, and his regime made less use of police power for political purposes than any previous Chilean regime, even that of the Christian Democrats. The press remained supremely and outrageously free, as did the universities, the trade unions and the other institutions which his opponents sought to pervert.

In his unrelenting pursuit over a lifetime of the power he recognized to be necessary to attain his objectives, he exhibited one of the major qualities of the professional politician. Another was visible in his ability to hold together in power his disparate coalition and retain the leadership and support of his own party even when he favored policies for which it had little liking. And beyond that he had an integrity which survived alike the blandishments of friends and the bribes and threats of foes, a readiness to die in defense of his dream, which raises him from the status of politician to that of statesman and national leader.

But probably the most important contribution of the Allende presidency to Chile was the awakening to understanding, among broad sectors of previously passive people, of the injustice of the system which oppressed them, and to the possibility of changing that system. The process did not start with the victory of the UP coalition, and it was fed by factors other than those introduced by the Allende government. But that government was an important catalyst. One can prophesy with considerable confidence that Chile will never be the same again.

The growth in class consciousness was quickly recognized by the traditional holders of power as the mortal threat to their domination which in fact it represents. A small minority can monopolize the benefits of a society only while it can prevent the majority from understanding the true facts of the situation. To do this it manipulates a broad range of institutions, including the legal and judicial systems, the law-enforcement police and military agencies, and the media of communications. All of these are geared to creating a high level of class consciousness (usually described as esprit-de-corps or "old school tie") in its own ranks, a range of subsidiary and supportive groups suitably rewardable and punishable, and a proletarian isolation of the masses from knowledge and from structured cooperation. The optimum functioning of the system calls for the minimizing of visible physical force and the maximizing of resigned acceptance of its inevitability through control of minds and imaginations.

The first significant, though still marginal, challenge to

the system came with the protests of the miners and other industrial and commercial workers late in the nineteenth century. As the economy became steadily more foreign-controlled and foreign-oriented during the twentieth century, with a corresponding increase in the inequality of rewards and benefits, the process intensified under the leadership of the Communist Party and the Socialist Party. The emotional mobilization of the masses was given additional impetus, especially in rural areas, during the 1960s by the Christian Democrats. They developed broad-based organizations, though generally within a paternalistic framework of control from above. The UP government speeded up the process significantly, each element in the coalition making its distinctive contribution. The Communist Party, bound by ideology and tradition, encouraged a paternalistic centralization of control similar to that sought by the Christian Democrats. Allende, with his quixotic commitment to constitutional processes, agreed with them. He feared that self-starting popular structures would make their own timetables without concern for legal niceties, as indeed some did. The Socialist Party and MAPU were more aware that a balance of power required that the people build their own power structures to match those already institutionalized. In this evaluation of the realities of power they were enthusiastically encouraged by the MIR militants of the far left.

By the middle of 1972, the power holders were seeing clearly that their control of the voting process by the traditional methods of manipulation of power was being eroded. An opinion survey of Santiago commissioned by the opposition-controlled *Ercilla* magazine in September 1972 showed that 60 percent of the people viewed the performance of the UP government favorably, and that a majority considered the strategies of the opposition to be harmful to the country. It also brought out the growing

191

class identification. The rich were solidly against the government, the middle classes divided, and the poor enthusiastic.[1] The March 1973 congressional elections confirmed the trend. The substantial growth of electoral backing for the UP coalition meant that only naked force could stop it. As Sergio Onofre Jarpa, president of the National Party, commented, "the struggle now is not in the ballot box but in the streets."

The Right had traditionally enjoyed private, vigilante-style armies. These were now rapidly expanded with outside arms, money and supplies. The external, dependent quality of this counter-revolutionary movement is striking, suggesting that the international conspiracy to control the world is to be sought in directions other than those usually indicated. The code name for the Fatherland and Freedom training center in Bolivia was *Operación Banderantes* (operation trail blazers), a translation of that used in Brazil by the regime-encouraged political assassins who have for several years been terrorizing the opponents of the military dictatorship. The plan to overthrow Allende was *Operación Djakarta*, the name suggested in 1970 by a United States transnational company executive. The subsequent "pacification" program has been studiously modeled on South Vietnam's search-and-destroy Operation Phoenix. Hardly coincidentally, the United States Ambassador in Santiago was Nathaniel P. Davis who headed the embassy in Guatemala from 1968 to 1971. With him in Santiago were many of the veterans of the Vietnam pacification whose Operation Phoenix had by 1971 left 20,000 dead in Guatemala. To build their international network of support, the Chilean plotters had private airplanes and sophisticated electronic equipment for meetings in Argentina, Bolivia, Brazil and the United States.

The growth of the armed power of the Right and its open use to eliminate the more conspicuous leaders of the slum-dwellers and peasants, as well as to promote the campaign of economic chaos by destroying bridges and electricity transmission lines, brought an inevitable response from the Left. Even before 1970, the MIR had urged its supporters to arm in self-defense, but—as indicated earlier—all available evidence indicates that the level was low. During the first half of 1973, however, the arming of sectors of the Left, expecially for the defense of the factories, progressed significantly, in part by clandestine importations, in part by "gifts" from sympathizers in the armed forces. Some attempts were made to build medium heavy weapons in factories, but the required expertize seems to have been lacking. However, following the universal pattern of contemporary guerrillas, the Left built up stocks of Molotov cocktails and other explosives, the materials being readily available in the mining camps. The arming of the Left, even including the presidential guard to which Allende entrusted his safety after he received in March 1973 conclusive evidence of major military plotting, never came near the level of the Right. It could have been significant only if the armed forces had split, a possibility seriously feared by the Right and prevented by the "coup before the coup" which purged the armed forces on the early morning of September 11.

The preventive strike within the armed forces was only a small part of the careful planning of the counter-revolution. Eduardo Frei and some of his associates welcomed the plotting because they naively believed that "normality" could and would be restored by a classical Latin American coup to substitute a malleable president for an intransigent one. The plotters were far more realistic. They knew they would never be safe unless they succeeded in eliminating the self-understanding newly acquired by the poor, and to do this, structures of oppression hitherto unknown to Chile would have to be created. Here again, their dependence and lack of originality are significant. The scenario follows literally the model unveiled in Brazil in 1964, and more recently introduced also to Bolivia and Uruguay. The major difference is in the level of oppression judged necessary in Chile. The institutionalization of arbitrary power reached in Brazil only after more than four years of experimentation was achieved in Chile in a few weeks. About 1,000 dissenters were killed in Brazil in nine years, a number probably reached in as many hours in Chile.

Examination of this Brazilian prototype, which President Nixon has offered to all Latin Americans as the direction they must ultimately follow, will help to understand what is now happening in Chile and what is to come. It reveals that the grand design is to return Chile to its former status as an economic satellite of Western capitalism, and more specifically of United States-based transnational corporations, but now under the iron grip of a military dictatorship equipped with the know-how and armaments needed to maintain order while the country's resources are being exploited for the benefit of a few at the expense of the impoverished majority. This will cause a recrudescence of the features of underdevelopment which the UP government sought to eliminate: a great disparity in productivity between urban and rural areas, a large majority of the people living at a physiological subsistence level, and constantly increasing masses of underemployed people in the urban zones.

That such a plan is already being implemented was stressed by the London-based *Latin America* three months after the take-over. It quoted a "Chilean economist with an international reputation" as saying that the economic program set out in *El Mercurio* "accurately reflects the views of the foreign business community," and that it can work only "if the population were reduced to six million." That would signify the literal Brazilianization of Chile by reducing 40 percent of its present population of ten million to the marginal condition in which 40 percent of Brazilians live, making no effective contribution to the gross national product and consuming only enough to subsist badly and die early of malnutrition-induced diseases.[2]

Like Chile more recently, Brazil had dreams of creating a just society by its own efforts. In 1955, President Juscelino Kubitschek initiated his term of office with an ambitious five-year "Target Plan" for self-sustained growth in energy, transport, food, basic industries and education, plus a new capital, Brasilia. The gross national product had grown nearly 30 percent in the previous five years, and Kubitschek achieved a further 41 percent through his plan. But the cost was high, a truce with the country's reactionary forces which left intact their ownership and exploitation of the rural-agricultural complex. As in Chile up to 1970, landownership was highly concentrated, and the landowners were concerned with power even before profit. They held the peasant 50 percent of the population at the traditional subsistence living levels, thus denying to expanding industry a potential market. The 12 percent rate of increase in urban demand for food was twice the growth rate of the food supply, causing such a price rise that the urban workers spent their entire income on food. Only one quarter of the population had any income left to buy industrial products.

Jánio Quadros and João Goulart, Kubitschek's successors, proposed the creation of farm cooperatives and state farms as a counterweight to the landowners. Many of the new industrialists were frightened by the state's growing role, and also by the high taxes and inflation resulting from the government's efforts to broaden its popular base. When business and the landowners united against him, Goulart appealed to the workers. He proposed radical policies of land and income redistribution, economic nationalism, nationalization of large sectors of production, political mobilization of the urban and rural masses, and international neutralism and nonalignment.

195

In March 1964 he signed a decree nationalizing the private oil refineries and a decree for land reform. They were his political death warrant. Encouraged by United States policy-makers who cut back sharply on aid to Brazil, a coalition of politicians, businessmen and military overthrew him on March 31. Public opinion had been prepared by massive demonstrations led by well-to-do women indoctrinated by retired generals in anti-communist propaganda. They recited the rosary as they marched, to save Brazil from the "Bolshevist peril." President Johnson did not even wait for Goulart to leave Brazil before according recognition to the new regime. Laws providing for distribution of land to peasants were rescinded. Regulations limiting export of business profits were cancelled and the oil refineries were denationalized, in return for promises of United States aid and investments. Congress was purged. Thousands were jailed and 2,000 military men were retired. Government nominees replaced the leaders of key trade unions. National and state unions of students were outlawed, and peasant leagues were disbanded, leaving Brazil as a textbook example of proletarianization through the elimination of all intermediate structures between the citizen and the state. Brazil had become what Brazilian political scientist Helio Jaguaribe has called a "colonial fascist" state: fascist, because it seeks "to promote economic development without changing the existing social order"; colonial, because it depends "on the West in general and the United States in particular, due to its need for foreign assistance and foreign markets."

Significant economic progress was quickly registered, and soon the regime was boasting of the "economic miracle" of steady growth of the gross national product at rates as high as ten percent annually. What it did not stress was that the progress was paid for by a cut in the purchasing power of the average worker's income to 60 percent of the already low levels of 1964, that the benefits were concentrated in the small upper class and their transnational allies, that the proportion of Brazilian industry controlled by the transnationals was each year bigger as Brazilian private enterprise was smothered in the unequal competition. Neither did they stress that the gap between the few rich and the many poor was wider each year than the year before, that the absolute level of the poverty of the many was lower, and that the number of unemployed Brazilians was higher. Nor did they stress that several efforts to relax controls and restore some of the forms of democracy had aborted, and that maintenance of the system called each year for greater oppression. The success of the policy may be measured by the fact that between 1960 and 1970 the percentage of the gross domestic product enjoyed by the richest one percent of Brazilians rose from 11.5 to 18.2, while the percentage shared by the poorest 50 percent fell from 17.8 to 14.3.

The only institution which the military dictatorship did not succeed in domesticating fully in Brazil was the church. During the previous reformist regimes, the Catholic church had openly encouraged the socially progressive policies of the government, and for two or three years after the establishment of the dictatorship in 1964, substantial elements in that church continued to express concern at the mounting oppression. Gradually, however, they were silenced by censorship and other measures. During those same years, guerrilla activities developed in many parts of the country, more particularly in the city and state of São Paulo, and various foci of resistance were also created in the backward rural parts of the Northeast and Amazonia. An upsurge of repression, involving wholesale torture of suspects and the organization of officially approved or condoned murder squads, following the institutionalization of completely arbitrary rule in 1968, stamped out all such efforts. Brazilians settled down to a long, dark night. Political observers were convinced that ultimately the underlying pressures would reach a point of explosion, but they recognized that the power in the hands of the oppressors—backed by the might of the United States—could delay that explosion for ten or fifteen years. In 1973, however, new dynamic factors began to manifest themselves. Brazilians in the power structures, both military men and representatives of business, began to question the economic policies. Of particular concern was the growth in the external debt to $15 billion, involving interests payments of nearly $2 billion. Criticism came from an unexpected source, when Robert McNamara, president of the World Bank, cited a study of the unsatisfactory distribution of income in Brazil to justify the bank's reluctance to grant loans to countries which did not use them to diminish social inequalities. And criticism of extraordinary vehemence and directness was voiced by the long-silent Catholic church, which bypassed the censorship of the media of communications by having the protests read in the churches and smuggled abroad for worldwide distribution. These statements are of vital importance, because the bishops used the tools of the social sciences to make an in-depth analysis of the effect of the economic and social policies being pursued in Brazil since 1964. The conclusion reached is that these policies, which are being pursued at the behest of international overlords, are anti-human and nonviable. The challenge is consequently to the approach to world development being promoted and financed by the United States. Its relevance to what has happened and what is now happening in Chile is immediate.

The criticism has been formalized in three long documents signed by the bishops of the Northeast, of the Center-West and of the Amazon. Each starts with an analysis of the specific area in which its signatories live, and all three reach substantially the same conclusions. The dictatorship, they say, is responsible not only for political repression and for physical tortures, but for poverty, starvation wages, unemployment, infant mortality and illiteracy. The international capitalist system is identified as the cause of this situation, and the military regime is presented as the instrument of domination for foreign capitalists allied with local oligarchs. Socialism, they add, is the only alternative if we are to construct "a world in which all antagonism of religion, class and race, and international aggression and exploitation" can be overcome.

The concentration of ownership of land and capital means that "the rich become always richer and the poor always poorer in the enslaving process of economic concentration inherent in the system." This in turn requires a regular growth in the level of repression: "curtailing the constitutional prerogatives of the legislative branch of government, the depoliticization of rural and urban trade unions; the elimination of student leadership; the establishment of censorship; persecution of workers, peasants and intellectuals; harassment of priests and members of active groups within the Christian churches—all this in various forms of imprisonment, torture, mutilation and assassination." As for the role of the United States, "international capitalism and its allies in our country—the dominant class—impose through the media of communication a dependent culture. . . . The historical process of class society and of capitalistic domination necessarily leads to a fatal confrontation of the classes. . . . The dominated class has no other road to freedom except the long and difficult trek now under way, in favor of social ownership of the means of production."[3]

Chile's military Junta has not only utilized the experience of Brazil but leapfrogged the early experimental stages of the Brazilian process. The army came into the streets, as General Pinochet had warned earlier, "to kill," and it quickly acquired the reputation of an army of occupation even among those who had most opposed the

UP government. Thousands of people suspected of being leaders of popular movements were systematically eliminated, factories which workers attempted to defend were destroyed, and communities regarded as centers of militancy were wiped out. All this was done within an organizational framework which made it clear, as was confirmed by other indications later, that the military plan had been fully perfected in advance. The conspirators had established contacts with the Brazilian military long before the revolt. Brazilians trained in the Panama Canal Zone had trained Chilean right-wing commandos in Bolivia. Immediately after the revolt, Brazilian security personnel flew into Santiago to join in interrogation of Brazilian exiles who had found asylum in Chile during the previous years.

The political institutionalization of the military was quickly effected. The constitution was abrogated and Congress dissolved. Municipal councils also were dissolved, and army officers were installed as mayors. All parties of the UP coalition and all parties which supported it were abolished. All other political parties were suspended indefinitely and political activities at all levels, from Congress down to local neighborhood organizations, were prohibited. The attacks on undesirables was quickly expanded by *El Mercurio*, which under the iron censorship can alone express opinions, to include the Christian Democrats. It reported, for example, that a "pro-marxist group" inside the Christian Democrats, led by Radomiro Tomic, Bernardo Leighton and Renán Fuentealba, was planning an underground organization to maintain contact with the dissolved UP parties, help those living in hiding, and blame the armed forces for the gathering economic chaos. In this way it hoped to secure early elections and remobilize the people to bring itself to power in those elections. What such tendentious reporting sought was to discredit the Christian Democrats and ensure total rightist control.[4] That this policy has in fact succeeded is the view of Professor

200

Laurence Birns of New York's New School for Social Research, a long-time student of Chile who spent several months there early in 1973 as consultant for an international organization, "The generals no longer lead a national army," he says, "as they did just a few weeks ago, but have now become the force of the *oligarquía*, the coalition of big business and big landowners that opposed not only Allende but the reforms of Frei as well. I suspect that at least 40 percent of the population despises them, a proportion that will grow as members of the middle class and the professions come more and more to resent the new arrogance of the military and the policies it is bound to pursue.[5]

Having armed itself with total power, the Junta presented the broad lines of its economic plans, again following the Brazilian model literally. It announced that it would return most of the more than 300 companies, about 40 of them with United States investment, which had been taken over by the Allende regime under the intervention law of 1932. These did not include the copper companies which had been nationalized by a constitutional amendment for which all parties had voted. Copper for Chile has acquired the same universal emotional significance as petroleum for Brazil, forcing the Junta to move cautiously. All it promised was to reopen negotiations on the issue of compensation, thus postponing the hard decisions but permitting the resumption of United States aid without loss of face on either side. It further insisted that its plans to revive the economy would "place priority on foreign investment."[6] The United States, for its part, used more finesse than usual. The first big loan to the Junta was from the government of Brazil, thereby avoiding a conflict in the United States Congress while the issue of repression in Chile was on the front pages, and increasing the leverage for the puppet Brazilian regime which is accorded by Washington the leadership of South America. The United

States banks which had cancelled credits to Chile quickly rushed back with all the short-term credits needed to conduct normal trade.

The Brazilian model was also used, but applied far more drastically, to cancel the benefits reaped by the poor during the previous three years, and to make them pay immediately for whatever losses the rich felt they had suffered. The first step was to eliminate food subsidies and close down the food-distribution centers in the poor districts. The 200 percent wage increase (to match inflation) decreed by the Allende government to take effect on October 1, 1973, was cancelled, while price controls on food and other necessities were eliminated. In spite of pessimistic reports given wide circulation by the opponents of Allende during the first half of 1973, reports which the United States Embassy in Santiago fed to foreign correspondents when it knew they were not correct, there was no real food shortage. Food available in Santiago was, on a per capita basis, 20 percent more in 1972 than in the last year of the Frei government, and in 1973 it was still 15 percent above the 1969-70 level. But government control of prices and distribution had given the poor a fairer share than under the old system of supply-and-demand. The return to that old system meant that the poor would again starve, while others would have a superabundance.[7]

The main thrust of all propaganda was directed to undoing the work of politicization among the workers, slum dwellers and peasants. The press, radio and television mounted a massive campaign of denigration of Allende and the other leaders designed to show that they had deceived their followers, living high while the poor starved, engaged in black-market activities, hoarding, gambling and loose living. House-to-house searches with tanks, machine guns and dogs were shown on television to demoralize resisters. The viewer saw and heard how "dangerous" men were isolated, stripped, checked for scars or wounds, with soldiers hitting them on chests and backs as they went down the line. A rat-on-your-neighbor campaign quickly created such a level of suspicion that people no longer talked to one another. Identified supporters of Allende were fired from their jobs, 1,000 miners from El Teniente alone, 500 workers at the state electricity company, 500 from the land reform administration, 400 from the central bank. Streets and buildings were renamed in an effort to wipe from memory the three years of Allende's rule. Even Gabriela Mistral, Chile's most famous poet after Pablo Neruda and unlike him not identified with leftist causes, was not spared. Allende had given her name to the elaborate building constructed for the meeting of UNCTAD in 1972, a building now being used as the seat of government until La Moneda is rebuilt. It has become the Diego Portales building to honor a statesman of the middle of the nineteenth century. The name may be symbolic. Portales welcomed the English merchants who soon made Chile a profitable exploitation area for English entrepreneurs.

As noted in the previous chapter, a purge of the country's universities opened the way for the Junta to remodel these basic Chilean institutions in their own anti-marxist perspective. As Colonel Eugenio Reyes, new rector of the State Technical University in Santiago, put it, "We are trying to apoliticize the universities, just as we are trying to apoliticize the country." This is fully in line with the Brazilian program which has destroyed all linkages within groups to make the individual wholly dependent on the state as expressed in the armed forces, and wholly isolated in his dealings with this supreme and unchallangeable authority.

The *poblaciones* which ring Santiago and house a quarter to a half of the city's nearly 4,000,000 inhabitants have been an area of major concern. They were the element of Chilean life which had responded most enthusiastically to the efforts of the UP government and its allies to politicize

203

their natural constituency. From their original condition of shantytowns, many had developed into integrated neighborhoods with simple but solid homes, and with previously unimagined facilities for food distribution, child and health care, and education for young and old. Now the leaders have been killed or imprisoned, or are in hiding. The food-distribution centers have been closed, as have the health centers and other community services.

With the church the Chilean Junta dealt more forcibly than the Brazilian generals ever attempted. Unlike Allende, who had rigorously avoided interference with church institutions, the Catholic University was treated like the other universities, a military man installed as rector in violation of a church-state agreement that the church authorities alone had this right. Along with other institutions dealing with social and political sciences, the Center of Studies of the National Reality, part of Catholic University, was closed down. The Catholic University was included in the suspension of schools or programs of sociology, social work, economics and journalism.

Foreign missionaries, both Catholic and Protestant, were listed as among the "dangerous" foreigners encouraged by the Allende regime to enter Chile and corrupt simple people with their marxist theories. Many of them did in fact work in the *poblaciones*, because most Chilean clergy preferred a more traditional ministry to people in a higher social and economic category. The Junta ordered that all foreign religious personnel be eliminated from the *poblaciones*. Many were arrested in the systematic searches by the army and several were killed. Others fled to embassies. About 60 percent of all Catholic priests in Chile are foreigners, and it is estimated that of these, two-thirds to the number of 500, have been or will be forced to leave, as well as many foreign nuns and Protestant missionaries who are judged sympathetic to the aspirations of the workers and peasants. The Junta is obviously determined not to

204

repeat the mistake made by the Brazilian generals when they left in place church structures around which an opposition could later re-form.

An indication of the extent to which the Junta is going was provided by the seizure of St. George's, a primary and secondary school in Santiago run for thirty years by Holy Cross priests from Notre Dame, Indiana. The school, with 2,600 pupils, was staffed by twelve Holy Cross priests, eight from the United States, and three nuns from Connecticut. It had long been one of the most prestigious schools for children of the rich in Santiago, and for several years parents had complained because the priests insisted on including in the curriculum some very mild courses outlining Catholic teaching on social issues, and also gave free tuition to a small number of children of workers. The complaints escalated after Allende's overthrow to charges of "marxist indoctrination and political activity," seizure of the school and expulsion of teachers and other staff members.

When public and private elementary and secondary schools reopened in October 1973, all texts that might predispose pupils to "certain ideologies" had been eliminated, and all subjects that might influence them "politically" had been suspended. To fill the gaps, Education Minister Admiral Hugo Castro had ordered additional courses in the history and geography of Chile.[8]

The Junta gave the highest priority to the elimination of opposition leadership, actual and potential. Many were hunted down and killed during the first weeks, not for overt acts committed by them either before or after the revolt, but simply because of their contribution to ideas and views now ruled subversive. Many other escaped across the border into Argentina or found aylum in friendly embassies or in the refugee centers established by international agencies, from which they later made their way abroad. Others would follow them when fired from their

205

jobs and denied the possibility of work at home. It was estimated that 15,000 Chileans would have fled before the exodus ended. Also driven from Chile were a further 10-15,000 Latin Americans who had in the previous ten years found haven there as political refugees from their homelands, with Brazilians, Bolivians and Uruguayans in the majority. Most were young intellectuals, many still students, the finest potential leadership in their respective countries. In Chile, they had found a congenial atmosphere in which to continue their studies, while planning and organizing to return home one day to a country in which it would be possible for them to contribute to economic, political and cultural progress.

Latin America has a tradition of political exile. Dictatorships in Haiti, Nicaragua and Paraguay are the norm. But in the past there were always places where victims of repression could recoup and reorganize. Today that is no longer true. Little more than a decade after the United States had joined with the other American republics in a solemn treaty "to improve and strengthen democratic institutions," the blight of military dictatorship has spread across the continent—Peru, Ecuador, Honduras, El Salvador, Argentina, the Dominican Republic, Brazil, Bolivia, Panama, Uruguay, and now Chile—with few protests and usually quick welcomes from Washington.

Argentina alone had reversed the trend, the determination of the majority finally forcing the military to permit a return to the government the people wanted. But even there, the balance remains doubtful. It is not a situation in which exiles could hope to duplicate the conditions they enjoyed in Chile. The atmosphere of Colombia is even more negative. Venezuela and Mexico alone remain, and neither offers an economic base for any significant number or an assurance that freedom of association, research and expression will continue indefinitely. What the exiles face is dispersion in the United States and Canada and across

Europe from France to Scandinavia. The receiving countries will undoubtedly benefit, but the dissipation and gradual absorption of Latin America's best brains means a loss the hemisphere cannot afford, a further giant step toward permanent satellitization and incorporation in the invisible empire.

The Junta has spoken frankly of its intention to retain dictatorial powers indefinitely. In ordering an end to previously authorized "summary executions" six weeks after it seized power, it insisted that this change did not mean that greater toleration would be shown to opponents. "War has been declared and we want to see it to the end," said General Oscar Bonilla Bradanovic, Minister of the Interior. General Pinochet, head of the Junta, said the military would retain control until "the country has achieved the social peace necessary for progress and economic development." The state of siege might be lifted in June 1974, he said, but the state of internal war would continue.[9]

The prospects of social peace while the Junta remains in power seem, however, remote. By driving all parties and groupings of the Left underground, and by eliminating the influence of other parties, especially the Christian Democrats who reflect a broad spectrum of centrist and center-left opinion, it has upset the balance of forces in a country in which that balance had long been delicately poised. All key positions are being filled by men of proven reactionary attitudes. The only holdovers are those who had clearly established their opposition to Allende, like Enrique Urrutia, president of the supreme court. Urrutia quickly defended the military seizure of power, because the Allende government had "lost its legitimacy," and because he trusted "the goodwill of the military leaders." In consequence, he had no objection to the dissolution of Congress, abolition of most political parties and suspension of the others, and the imposition of censorship.[10]

The values of the Junta are those of the Fatherland and Freedom movement, headed by Pablo Rodríguez who has been described by Richard Gott of the *Manchester Guardian* as "a Fascist in a familiar European mold using words like 'integral' and 'corporative' without batting an eyelid."[11] Roberto Thieme, closest associate of Rodríguez as secretary general of Fatherland and Freedom, is son of a Nazi storm trooper and apes his father's style. The Junta quickly released him from jail where he was held on charges of subversion of the armed forces, sabotage and the illegal possession of arms. He had boasted openly of his part in the unsuccessful tank attack on La Moneda in June 1973. Jaime Guzmán, the most influential of the eight men who have been commissioned to draft a new constitution in secret, thinks like Rodríguez. He has let it be known that the *gremios* (employer associations) will have a "decisive" voice in the new Congress. Before 1970, these employer associations played a determining, if informal, role as lobbyists with Congress and the administration, something like the National Association of Manufacturers and the National Rifle Association in Washington. They turned against Allende when they found they could not manipulate him, organizing the economic chaos which brought him down. Now they want to be rewarded by having their traditional role openly institutionalized, and the Junta shows every intention of complying. Admiral Hugo Castro, named education minister after he had demonstrated his zeal as a book burner at the Technical University of Valparaíso, says his objective is to destroy marxism first, then "every kind of politics." The Santiago press, without humor and apparently without irony, stressed Castro's outstanding qualifications for his ministerial tasks: he had graduated from special courses—in the United States—in artillery, combat communications, torpedoes and sonar. Other spokesmen for the Junta parrot the Fatherland and Freedom slogans of "purity of the military movement," stopping "foreign ideologies" and the "communist cancer," returning to "nationalism," and eliminating "the poison of political awareness." The importance of "political awareness" is twofold. The oligarchs, as already noted, realize that the process of conscientizing and politicizing the workers and peasants constituted the ultimate threat to their monopoly of power and will do everything they can to reverse it. In addition, they think of themselves as being apolitical, outside and above politics. Their folk memory is of a past golden age when students, workers and peasants knew their place and took orders unquestioningly from those born to rule. Under such leaders as Rodríguez and Guzmán, they believe they can restore that past by creating a "corporate state" in the Spanish and Portuguese mould. This state is to be brought into existence, not by the action of the people either through their elected representatives or by submission of the constitution now being drafted to a referendum, but by decree of the military leaders. The legislative bodies to be created by this constitution will include, in addition to representatives of the *gremios*, a "continuing role" for the armed forces.[12]

The policy of containment encouraged and supported by the United States has achieved its primary purpose everywhere in Latin America for more than a decade. The guerrilla movements which mushroomed after the Castro victory in Cuba are not an immediate threat to any of the dictatorial regimes, not even in Uruguay. A fascist regime backed fully by the United States can maintain order in Chile for some considerable time. But the level of repression will have to remain extremely high. Chile has a much greater sense of self-identification and social cohesion among workers and peasants than Brazil. In addition, it seems clear that all the killing and imprisonment has not destroyed the organization of the opposition. A member of the Junta reported officially in October that the opposition has held "a clandestine congress," apparently a reference to an all-day meeting of the leaders of the parties of the UP coalition held some days after the overthrow. The conclusion of this meeting was reportedly that the MIR had been correct in its analysis that the parliamentary road to socialism was unrealistic, and that even the Communist Party, previously the most insistent on seeking compromises, was now ready to join with MIR in more violent tactics involving rural and urban guerillas.

Emergence of MIR as the recognized leader of the underground gives particular significance to an interview given by its leaders in early October to a French newspaper.[13] The MIR leaders claimed that they had clearly foreseen the military takeover and were "politically and organizationally" prepared for it. The Right had to resort to force, they said, because of a new factor which had just emerged, "a mobilization and heightening of consciousness among the Chilean workers which was totally new, having no common measure with anything that had transpired before." This process had been promoted by militants of the Socialist Party as well as by those of MIR, and it was paralleled by similar activities within the armed forces. While ultra elements are now in total control, the armed forces will not fail to reflect "the very real divisions which exist in the bourgeoisie." Certain regiments whose reliability was questioned did not participate in the house searches and repression. "Fragmentary evidence indicates quite a few refusals to obey on the part of certain soldiers and sub-officers. They were all shot immediately. . . . If there were a political and military revolutionary offensive which appeared as a real alternative, a good number of sub-officers and soldiers would be on our side." Because of this, MIR will avoid irresponsible acts that might cement the armed forces into a homogeneous block and will work to encourage "the slight but significant manifestations of resistance within the army."

Although the MIR calculations put at 25,000 the number of deaths in the battles for the factories during the five days after the revolt, "the revolutionary organizations—ours in particular—have not been dismantled. . . . The military know this, and it bothers them terribly. Their victory communiqués are tainted by an undercurrent of fear." MAPU also escaped serious damage either in organization or structure. The Communist Party lost many middle leaders, and it suffered disorientation because of the total failure of its long-pursued policy of compromise. The Socialist Party had many currents within it, and its more militant elements are preparing for future struggle.

Other sources confirm the MIR analysis and projection. The *rotos* (broken ones), says Professor Laurence Birns of the New School for Social Research, "had, during Allende's regime, lost the habit of accepting invisibility. Having tasted the real power that their government gave them, they cannot be expected to return to their former degradation. They too can kill. At the very least they can produce a Northern Ireland. They can bomb, they can kidnap, and they can assassinate. No military force is large enough to prevent this."[14] The underground newsletter *Between the Lines* is of the same opinion. Its issue dated November 1, 1973, reported that headlines and articles in the newspapers for the previous week suggested a fear on the part of the Junta of a coming counteroffensive from the Left. Two weeks later it reported that resistance continued. Having noted that a quarter of the Chilean air force had been eliminated in the first days of fighting after the revolt, with helicopters shot down as they attacked the *poblaciones* and several Hawker Hunter aircraft destroyed by saboteurs on the ground, it added that assaults against police patrols were still common in the south, and that an entire military regiment had been attacked on November 12. It also gave news of an underground newspaper which reported on the activities of the *Comandos Operativo del*

Pueblo, (people's army). "The possibilities for resistance in Chile to a long military dictatorship are real," it added, "and signs of hope are already beginning to appear." Another long-term threat to Chile's colonial fascism is the growing world awareness. Everywhere people are becoming conscious of the injustice of the present world order, and the network of communication and information bypassing the mass media controlled by the oppressors is being steadily perfected. The recent events in Chile show the power and ruthlessness of a system which sacrifices humans for gain, but the fact that power has to reveal itself in such raw terms is a warning that its limits are being approached.

That the day of reckoning will come for this inhuman system is not merely an expression of human hope but a reading of fully visible signs. That the struggle of the people has begun in earnest is the content of one of President Allende's last public statements. "What matters is to preserve the continuity of the revolutionary process," he said, "a process in which the people of Chile are the protagonists." The Junta smashed the political parties in the hope of delaying that process. They may well be hastening it instead by freeing the people from the assumptions and conventions of earlier politics and forcing them to rely on their own strength.

NOTES

Introduction

1. Raúl González Alvaro, editor of right-wing *Tribuna; New York Times*, Oct. 9, 1973.
2. Renato Poblete, "The Church and Social Change in Chile," *The Month*, London, Oct. 1973, quoting surveys made by church officials in the early 1960s.
3. *Documentos finales de Medellin.* (Buenos Aires: Ediciones Paulinas, 1969, p. 50).
4. Letter of Pope Paul VI to Cardinal Maurice Roy of Quebec, on 80th anniversary of Leo XIII's *Rerum Novarum*, May 1971.
5. Thomas Bamat, "Chile: Revolutionary Consciousness and the Peasantry," unpublished paper, Sociology Dept. Rutgers University, New Brunswick, N.J. 08903, 1973.
6. James F. Petras, "Nationalization, Socio-Economic Change and Popular Participation," *Studies in Comparative International Development*, Rutgers University, N.J., Vol. 8, No. 1, 1973.

Notes to Chapter 1

1. Jorge Ahumada, *En vez de la miseria.* Santiago de Chile: Editorial del Pacífico, 1958 and 1960, p. 16.
2. Preston E. James, *Latin America.* New York: Odyssey Press, 1950, p. 218.
3. Gary MacEoin, *Latin America: the Eleventh Hour.* New York: P.J. Kenedy, 1962, p. 37.
4. Chile Copper Corporation statement in *New York Times*, Jan. 25, 1971, and in Dale L. Johnson ed. *The Chilean Road to Socialism.* New York: Anchor Press/Doubleday, 1973, p. 101. Analysis of

profitability given by Carlos Fortin of Chile Copper Corporation to American Bar Association, May 4, 1973.
  5. Johnson ed. *The Chilean Road to Socialism*, p. 3.
  6. David E. Mutchler, *The Church as a Political Factor in Latin America: with Particular Reference to Colombia and Chile*. New York: Praeger, 1971, Chapters 12 to 15.
  7. Cited in James Petras: *Politics and Social Forces in Chilean Development*. Berkeley: University of California Press, 1969, pp. 107-8.
  8. Keith Griffin, *Underdevelopment in Spanish America*. Cambridge, Mass., MIT Press, 1970, p. 164.
  9. Andrew Zimbalist, "Dependence and Underdevelopment in Chile": unpublished paper, Harvard University, January 1971, pp. 32-33.
  10. *The Economist for Latin America*, Feb. 23, 1968, p. 11.
  11. Maurice Zeitlin, Lynda Ann Ewen and Richard Ratcliff, *Landlords and Capitalists*. New York: Harper and Row, 1973; quoted by Johnson, *The Chilean Road* . . . , p. 19.
  12. Johnson, *The Chilean Road* . . . , p. 20.
  13. David J. Morris, *We Must Make Haste—Slowly*. New York: Random House, 1973, p. 64. Morris gives as his source Gregorio Samsa, "Los salarios Actuales Son Menos de la Mitad de los del Año 1956," *Causa ML*, Oct. 1969, pp. 17-18.

Notes to Chapter 2.

  1. Quoted by David J. Morris, *We Must Make Haste—Slowly*, p. 87.
  2. On changing Catholic attitudes to Marxism in Latin America, see Gary MacEoin, "Marx with a Latin Beat," *Cross Currents*, Summer 1971, XXI, 3, p. 269.
  3. Morris, *We Must Make Haste—Slowly*, p. 32.
  4. David E. Mutchler, *The Church as a Political Factor in Latin America*, Chapters 12 to 15.
  5. Letter from Robert Berrellez (ITT, Buenos Aires) to Hendrix dated Sept. 29, 1970, quoted in IDOC, International Documentation Center, Quick Communications Service, #8, 1972, Rome, Italy.
  6. No action by the Justice Department followed.
  7. Johnson ed., *The Chilean Road* . . . , p. 149.
  8. NACLA, *New Chile*. Berkeley, Cal., and New York: North American Congress on Latin America, 1972, p. 137.
  9. Thomas Bamat and others. "Chile: New Road to a Socialist Society?" in *Cross Currents*, New York, Summer 1971, XXI, 3, p. 341.

10. Johnson ed., *The Chilean Road* . . . , p. 151.
11. Morris, *We Must Make Haste—Slowly*, p. 111.
12. ibid., p. 113.

1. David J. Morris, *We Must Make Haste—Slowly*, p. 107.
2. ibid., p. 186.
3. ibid., p. 196.
4. Johnson ed., *The Chilean Road* . . . , p. 33.
5. *New York Times*, Feb. 3, 1971.
6. Encyclopaedia Britannica, art. "Nationalization." Vol. XVI, 64, Chicago, 1973
7. Columbia Encyclopedia, art. "Nationalization." New York: Columbia University Press, third edition, 1963, p. 1460.
8. *New York Times*, Oct. 23 and Oct. 24, 1971.
9. *New York Times*, March 2, 1971.
10. *New York Times*, Feb. 3, 1971.
11. Report by Benjamin Welles, *New York Times*, Oct. 23, 1971. Other data about company maneuvers from Johnson ed., *The Chilean Road* . . . , pp. 50 and 112; NACLA, *New Chile*, p. 22.
12. *United States Foreign Aid in Action: a Case Study.* U.S. Senate, Committee on Government Operations, Subcommittee on Foreign Aid Expenditures, report by Sen. Ernest Gruening. Washington, D.C.: U.S. Government Printing Office, 1966, p. 2.
13. Inter-American Development Bank. *Socio-Economic Progress in Latin America.* Washington, D.C., 1971, p. 150.
14. *New York Times*, March 24, 1971.
15. *New York Times*, Aug. 12, 1971; *Wall Street Journal*, June 4, 1971; *National Catholic Reporter*, Oct. 12, 1973; *New Chile*, p. 46.
16. *New Chile*, p. 46.
17. *Barron's*, Oct. 23, 1972.
18. *National Catholic Reporter*, Oct. 12, 1973. *New Chile*, p. 49, gives total of IADB loans as $254 million.
19. *National Catholic Reporter*, Oct. 12, 1973. For AIFLD and the CIA, see Gary MacEoin, *Revolution Next Door.* New York: Holt, Rinehart and Winston, 1971, pp. 172-175.
20. *New Chile*, p. 48; *National Catholic Reporter*, Oct. 12, 1973.

Notes to Chapter 4

1. Norman Gall in *New York Times Magazine*, November 1, 1970.
2. *New York Times*, Sept. 17, 1970.

3. *Christian Science Monitor,* March 25, 1971; *New York Times,* March 12, 1971; *Washington Post,* June 21, 1971; *Der Spiegel,* August 31, 1971, p. 72; NACLA, *New Chile,* 1972, p. 117.

4. Jacques Chonchol in *New York Times,* Jan. 25, 1971.

5. David J. Morris, *We Must Make Haste—Slowly,* p. 125.

6. *New York Times,* April 1, 1973.

7. *Washington Post,* April 3, 1971.

8. Morris, *We Must Make Haste—Slowly,* p. 149.

9. *Los Angeles Times,* April 2, 1971; *Miami Herald,* April 6, 1971.

10. Christians for Socialism. Washington, D. C. [1500 Farragut St., N.W., 20011]: *Ecumenical Program for Inter-American Communication and Action,* 1973, p. 9.

11. Christians for Socialism, p. 10.

12. *Miami Herald,* July 16, 1971.

13. Armand Mattelart, "Estructura del Poder Informativo y Dependencia," *Cuadernos de la Realidad Nacional,* No. 3, Santiago de Chile, March 1970.

14. NACLA's *Latin American and Empire Report,* VII, 8, October 1973, p. 21.

15. *Miami Herald,* Oct. 30, 1971.

16. *New York Times,* Jan. 31, 1971.

17. *New York Times,* Oct. 3, 1971.

18. NC News Service, in *Catholic Herald,* Sacramento, Cal., Sept. 20, 1973. For Poblete's activities, see David E. Mutchler, *The Church as a Political Factor in Latin America, With Particular Reference to Colombia and Chile.* New York: Praeger, 1971, Chapters 12 to 15.

19. *Miami Herald,* Jan. 21, 1972.

20. *Miami Herald,* April 20, 1972.

21. *New York Times,* August 11, 1973.

22. *Manchester Guardian/Le Monde,* Sept. 15, 1973.

23. Morris, *We Must Make Haste—Slowly,* p. 262.

24. *Washington Post,* Jan. 29, 1971.

25. *Information Service on Latin America,* P.O. Box 4267, Berkeley, Cal. 94704.

26. *New York Times,* Oct. 4, 1972.

27. *New York Times,* July 2, 1971; *Newsweek,* Jan. 31, 1972, p. 33; *Miami Herald,* Dec. 16, 1970.

28. John C. Pollock and David Eisenhower, "The New Cold War in Latin America: the U.S. Press and Chile," in Johnson, *The Chilean Road . . . ,* pp. 71-86; Pollock, "What the Press Leaves Out," *The Nation,* Jan. 29, 1973, 134-138; John C. Pollock and Michele R. Pollock, "The U.S./Press and Chile: Ideology and International Con-

flict," Andover, Mass.: Warner Modules, Inc., 1974; John C. Pollock, Torry Dickinson and Joseph Somma, "Did Eichmann Have a Sense of Humor? The *New York Times* and Militarism in Chile," *The Latin American Studies Association Newsletter*, IV, 4, Dec. 1973.

29. *Miami Herald*, April 20, 1972.

Notes to Chapter 5

1. PARA, *Adentro Afuera*, # 14, July 1973, p. 7; *Miami Herald*, Feb. 20, 1972; *Manchester Guardian/Le Monde*, May 6, 1972.
2. PARA, *Adentro Afuera*, # 14, p. 8.
3. ibid., p. 8.
4. ibid., p. 22.
5. James Petras, *Politics and Social Structures in Latin America*. New York: Monthly Review Press, 1971.
6. "Statement on Chile," *Center of Concern*, 3700 13th Street, N.E., Washington, D.C. 20017, Sept. 1973.
7. *Latin America*, London, Dec. 1, 1972; *New York Times*, Nov. 10, 1971.
8. *New York Times*, Nov. 10, 1971 and Feb. 19, 1972.
9. *New York Times*, Dec. 1, 1971.
10. *New York Times*, Feb. 18 and 19, 1972; *Washington Post*, Feb. 19, 1972.
11. *Wall Street Journal*, Feb. 7, 1972; *Miami Herald*, March 5, 1972; *Washington Post*, March 18, 1972.
12. *Washington Post*, April 18, 1972; *New York Times*, April 20, 1972.
13. *Wall Street Journal*, Sept. 24, 1971; *Washington Post*, Sept. 26, 1971; *New York Times*, March 23, 1972; *Miami Herald*, March 31, 1972; *Los Angeles Times*, April 5, 1972; *Washington Post*, April 10, 1972. See also Anthony Sampson, *The Sovereign State of ITT*. New York: Stein and Day, 1973.
14. Joseph Collins. *National Catholic Reporter*, Kansas City, Mo., Oct. 12, 1973.
15. The terms of the treaty and the history of the negotiations are contained in a memorandum sent to Senator J.W. Fulbright, chairman of the Committee on Foreign Relations, and other United States senators and congressmen, in June 1973. The covering letter, dated June 7, 1973, is signed by Charles Curry, Patricia Ahern, Margaret Schuler, Thomas O'Brien, Joseph Eldridge and Raymond Plankey, as the coordination commission of PARA (U.S. Christians in Chile).
16. *Informations Catholiques Internationales*, Paris, # 441, Oct. 1, 1973, p. 9; PARA, *Adentro Afuera*, # 14, July 1973, p. 20; *Latin*

America, London, Oct. 20, 1972.
17. "Chile: the Story Behind the Coup," *Latin America Report*, VII, 8, p. 5, Oct. 1973. New York: NACLA.
18. *Latin America*, London, Jan. 19 and 26, 1973.
19. NC News Service, in *Catholic Herald*, Sacramento, Cal., Sept. 20, 1973.
20. *Latin America*, London, Feb. 9 and 16; March 9, 1972.

Notes to Chapter 6

1. PARA, *Adentro Afuera*, #13, May 1973, pp. 1-6.
2. PARA, *Adentro Afuera*, #14, July 1973, p. 11.
3. Report dated July 1973 from Fuente de Información Norteamericana, a research and publishing group of North Americans in Chile, which worked closely with United States Christians in Chile, in NACLA's *Latin American Report*, VII, 8, p. 24, October 1973.
4. *Labor Policies and Programs*, Subcommittee on American Republic Affairs, Committee on Foreign Relations, U.S. Senate, July 15, 1968, p. 4; Serafino Romualdi, *Presidents and Peons, Recollections of a Labor Ambassador in Latin America*. New York: Funk and Wagnalls, 1967, pp. 345-354.
5. "An Address by J. Peter Grace," printed in booklet form by the AIFLD, Sept. 16, 1965.
6. William Pfaff, in *Commentary*, New York, Jan. 1970. For a fuller discussion of this theme, see Gary MacEoin, *Revolution Next Door: Latin America in the 1970s*. New York: Holt, Rinehart and Winston, 1971, pp. 141 ss.
7. *New York Times*, Sept. 28, 1973.
8. MacEoin, *Revolution Next Door*, p. 143.
9. *New York Times*, Oct. 23, 1973.
10. Alain Joxe, *Las Fuerzas Armadas en el Sistema Politico Chileno*. Santiago: Editorial Universitaria, 1970, pp. 40-43.
11. *Miami Herald*, Oct. 28, 1971.
12. *Miami Herald*, March 28, 1972.
13. PARA, *Adentro Afuera*, #14, July 1973, p. 17.
14. *Washington Post*, April 3 and 7, 1973. When it shortly became known that Allende had wanted to keep the three military men in his cabinet but they refused, the move was understandably interpreted differently, as encouraging for the opposition. *Latin America*, April 6, 1973.
15. *Le Monde/Manchester Guardian*, April 7 and May 5, 1973; *Latin America*, April 6, 1973.
16. *Latin America*, April 6 and 13, 1973.

17. *Latin America,* April 13, 1973.
18. Religious News Service, New York, Sept. 12, 1973; *New York Times,* Aug. 29, 1973.

Notes to Chapter 7

1. *Washington Post,* Sept. 6, 1973.
2. *Latin America,* Nov. 9, 1973.
3. *Latin America,* Sept. 14 and 21, 1973.
4. *Manchester Guardian/Le Monde,* Sept. 8, 1973.
5. *Washington Post,* Sept. 9, 1973.
6. Agencia Arauco, Buenos Aires.
7. Taped account of Allende's death by eyewitness Luis Renato González Córdoba made in Mexican Embassy, Santiago, Sept. 15, 1973, brought from Chile by Fernanda Navarro, secretary to the President's widow [Hortensia Bussi de Allende], and published in University Review, New York, # 33, December 1973. In addition to the regular news sources, this chapter relies heavily on accounts provided the author by United States missionaries and graduate students who were in Chile at the time of the coup, refugees who have since left Chile, and members of various official missions who have since visited Chile.
8. *Manchester Guardian/Le Monde,* Sept. 15, 1973.
9. *Washington Post,* Sept. 23 and 25, 1973.
10. *Between the Lines,* Vol. I, No. 8, dated Nov. 1, 1973. The authenticity of its information is guaranteed not only by its internal consistency and specificity, but by the quality and reliability of the intermediaries through whom it came to the author of this book. Other data on church reaction to the revolt are from *Informations Catholiques Internationales,* Paris, Oct. 1 and 15, Nov. 1 and 15, 1973; and from *Vida Nueva,* Madrid, Nov. 17, 1973. *Vida Nueva* claims that Silva never said that the Pope was misinformed, that the statement was made by Junta members after they talked to Silva.
11. The document is dated October 1972 and signed by Baldo Santi M., vice-president of Caritas-Chile.
12. *Between the Lines,* Vol. I, No. 9, Nov. 8-15, 1973.
13. *Newsweek,* Oct. 8, 1973.
14. *Washington Post,* Sept. 7, Oct. 1, Oct. 3, 1973.
15. Mario Rinvolucri, *La Opinión,* Buenos Aires, Oct. 3, 1973.
16. Extract from written statement of Adam and Pat Garrett-Schesch presented at hearing of U.S. Senate subcommittee on refugees, Sept. 28, 1973, in *Refugee and Humanitarian Problems in Chile.* Washington: U.S. Government Printing Office, 1973, p. 19.

17. *Between the Lines,* Vol. I, No. 9, dated Nov. 8-15, 1973. For contemporary use of torture in interrogating suspects and the Pentagon's role therein, see Rona M. Fields, "Ulster: a Psychological Experiment?", *New Humanist,* March 1973.
18. *Between the Lines,* Vol. I, No. 8, dated Nov. 1, 1973.
19. Tad Szulc, *Washington Post,* Oct. 21, 1973. Szulc says he had read the secret testimony given on Oct. 10.
20. *Congressional Record,* Vol. 119, No. 143, Sept. 27, 1973.
21. *Chile Newsletter,* (Non-intervention in Chile, D.O.B 800, Berkeley, Cal., 96701) Vol. 1, No. 1, Nov. 1, 1973.
22. *Between the Lines,* Vol. 1, # 8, Nov. 1, 1973.
23. *New York Times,* Sept. 29, 1973.

Notes to Chapter 8

1. *New York Times,* Nov. 30, 1972.
2. *Latin America,* VII, 49, Dec. 7, 1973.
3. For Brazil since 1964, see Gary MacEoin, *Revolution Next Door: Latin America in the 1970s.* New York: Holt, Rinehart & Winston, 1971, pp. 183-205; Charles Antoine, *Church and Power in Brazil.* Maryknoll, N.Y.: Orbis Books, 1973; Celso Furtado, "The Post-1964 Brazilian 'Model' of Development," *Studies in Comparative International Development,* Rutgers University, New Jersey, Vol. 8, No. 2, Summer 1973, pp. 115-127. Figures on changes in income distribution, ISAL, *Pasos,* Santiago, Chile, No. 44, Feb. 4, 1973. For recent church criticisms, see *Latin America,* VII, 42, Oct. 19, 1973. Text of Northeast bishops' statement, IDOC North America, New York, No. 54, Summer 1973. Summary of the three episcopal statements, *Brazilian Information Bulletin,* No. 11, Fall 1973, P.O. Box 2279, Station A, Berkeley, Cal. 94702.
4. *Latin America,* VII, 48, Nov. 30, 1973.
5. *New York Review,* Nov. 1, 1973, p. 32.
6. *Journal of Commerce,* Sept. 28, 1973.
7. *Latin America,* VII, 41, Oct. 12, 1973.
8. *Washington Post,* Oct. 2, 1973.
9. *Latin America,* VII, 45, Nov. 9, 1973
10. *New York Times,* Oct. 18, 1973.
11. *Manchester Guardian/Le Monde,* Oct. 6, 1973.
12. *New York Times,* Sept. 22, 1973.
13. *Rouge,* No. 223, Oct. 5, 1973. English version in *URLA Newsletter,* Vol. 4, No. 1, Oct. 1973; 2205 San Antonio, Austin, Texas 78705.
14. *New York Review,* Nov. 1, 1973, p. 32.

BIBLIOGRAPHY

ALLENDE, SALVADOR. *Chile's Road to Socialism.* West Drayton, Middlesex: Penguin Books, 1974.
Competent and representative collection of Allende's political theories and social goals.

ANGELL, ALAN. *Politics and the Labor Movement in Chile.* New York and London: Oxford University Press, 1972.
Valuable statistical and other empirical evidence of growth of labor movement and long struggle for its control between Communist Party and Socialist Party, and later efforts of Christian Democrats to get a foothold.

COCKCROFT, JAMES D., ANDRÉ GUNDER FRANK and DALE L. JOHNSON. *Dependence and Underdevelopment: Latin America's Political Economy.* New York: Anchor Books/Doubleday, 1972.
This collection of radical analyses by leading social scientists includes several chapters dealing specifically with Chile, with particular attention to class structures and class attitudes.

COFFLA. *Chile: Unmasking Development.* Washington, D.C. (1500 Farragut Street, N.W.), 1973.
Packet of informative articles from many sources intended as an organizing tool and resource kit for group discussions. Challenges the "American Way" as a model for Third World development. COFFLA

221

is a radical group in the NACLA tradition, with input from missionary sources and strong religious motivation. ($2.50 postpaid).

DEBRAY, REGIS. *The Chilean Revolution: Conversations with Allende.* New York: Vintage, 1972.
French journalist, a marxist, recently released from a Bolivian prison in which he had been held as an associate of Che Guevara, argues at length with Allende that socialism cannot be established in Chile or anywhere by peaceful means.

FEINBERG, RICHARD. *The Triumph of Allende: Chile's Legal Revolution.* New York: Mentor, 1972.
Sympathetic overview of Chilean situation which led to Allende's 1970 electoral success, and optimistic description of the period immediately following. Fails to recognize depth of United States resistance to the experiment and consequently makes projections which events have hopelessly negatived.

JOHNSON, DALE L., ed. *The Chilean Road to Socialism.* New York: Anchor Books/Doubleday, 1973.
This symposium surveys many aspects of work of the Allende regime from the viewpoint of admirers, including land reform, nationalization of copper, and politicizing of workers and peasants. Much excellent material, but some of minor value.

JOXE, ALAIN. *Las fuerzas armadas en el sistema político de Chile.* Santiago de Chile: Editorial Universitaria, 1970.
Important particularly because it explodes the widely held view that the armed forces have been traditionally and consistently outside politics. English summary in *Monthly Review,* New York, January 1970.

KAUFMAN, ROBERT R. *The Politics of Land Reform in Chile.* Cambridge, Mass.: Harvard University Press, 1972.
Evaluates new forces brought into play by land reform, including ideological and political conflicts between different categories of peasants encouraged by landowners seeking to frustrate reform.

LAU, STEPHEN F. *The Chilean Response to Foreign Investment.*

New York: Praeger, 1972.
Detailed analysis of attitudes of different political groups to Chilean policy governing foreign investment.

MACEOIN, GARY. *Revolution Next Door: Latin America in the 1970s.* New York: Holt, Rinehart and Winston, 1971.
Overview of hemispheric pressures and counterpressures which brought Allende to power only to overthrow him.

MORRIS, DAVID J. *We Must Make Haste Slowly: the Process of Revolution in Chile.* New York: Random House, 1973.
A United States graduate student in Chile, impressed by UP regime's effort to progress without violence, gives the non-scholar the elements he needs to make his own judgments.

MOSS, ROBERT. *Chile's Marxist Experiment.* London: David and Charles, 1973.
A staff writer for the London *Economist*, a publication as reactionary as Chile's *El Mercurio*, Moss formulates the oligarchy's version of the rise and fall of Allende.

MUTCHLER, DAVID E. *The Church as a Political Factor in Latin America, with particular reference to Colombia and Chile.* New York: Prager, 1971.
Valuable data on part played by Chile's church leaders in bringing the Christian Democrats to power in 1964, and their embarrassment when the UP coalition triumphed in 1970.

NACLA. *New Chile.* New York: North American Congress on Latin America, 1973.
Tables and articles which help identify the patterns and processes of United States influence in Chile as expressed in the military, trade-union and business spheres. Brings out the overwhelming dependence of Chile on external decision-makers and thus offers background for understanding the dynamics of the counterrevolution.

NACLA. *News Letter.* "Chile: Special Issue," March 1971; "Secret Memos from ITT," April 1972; "There Will be Work for All," September 1972; "Chile: Facing the Blockade," January 1973; "Chile: the Story Behind the Coup," October 1973. The North

American Congress for Latin America, a closely-knit and ideological-
ly homogeneous team of political scientists, sociologists and cultural
historians, clustered around (but independent of) Columbia University, New York, and Berkeley, California, has pioneered in offering a
radical re-evaluation of the United States impact on Latin America.
Solidly documented, logical in analysis.

NICH. *Chile Newsletter.* Box 800, Berkeley, Cal. 94701.
"Non-Intervention in Chile," a group formed in 1972 to study
United States involvement in Chile, started in November 1973 to
publish a monthly report offering radical interpretations.

PETRAS, JAMES. *Politics and Social Forces in Chilean Development.* University of California Press, 1969.
Documented analysis by informed social scientist of political
parties and developments in political activity in Chile during the
1960s.

——————, and HUGO ZEMELMAN MERINO. *Peasants in Revolt: a
Case Study, 1965-71.* Austin, Texas, and London: University of
Texas Press, 1972.
Important case study of the processes of politicization spurred by
the Chilean land reforms.

TOURAINE, ALAIN. *Vie et Mort du Chili Populaire.* Paris: Seuil,
1973. French sociologist's diary, written in Chile July 29 to September 24, 1973, a day-to-day analysis of forces and events. Important.

ZAMMIT, J. ANN, ed. *The Chilean Road to Socialism.* Austin,
Texas; University of Texas Press; Sussex, England: Institute of
Development Studies, 1973.
Proceedings of major conference organized in Santiago in March
1972 by Chilean National Planning Office and Sussex Institute of
Development Studies. Sections cover macro-economic and industrial
policy; land policy, foreign policy and external sector problems;
participation and socialist consciousness; prospects for the UP government; the Chilean road to socialism. Also included are papers on
experiments in socialist transformation in Tanzania, Yugoslavia,
Cuba, and Hungary. Excellent reference book and bibliography.

224

INDEX

229